M000311221

EMBRACING FAILURE

EMBRACING
Failure

Harness the Power of Fear
in Life and Business

MAT PELLETIER

LIONCREST
PUBLISHING

EMBRACING FAILURE
Harness the Power of Fear in Life and Business

ISBN   978-1-5445-0330-1   *Hardcover*

978-1-5445-0328-8   *Paperback*

978-1-5445-0329-5   *Ebook*

This book is dedicated to my wife, Tami, who has saved my life on more than one occasion. Without her selfless support, none of my accomplishments would have been possible. The inspiration for this book was derived from my two sons, Mathieu Jr. and Michael, who are proof that mankind and all humanity's best days lie ahead and are not in the past.

CONTENTS

INTRODUCTION

STARING DOWN FAILURE

Matthew Webb was a steamship captain in Britain when he decided to be the first person to swim across the English Channel. Another man had recently attempted the crossing and failed, but Webb was confident he could complete the twenty-one-mile swim despite the icy water and unpredictable tides. He left his job, began training, and early one morning in 1875 he set out from Dover, England.

He swam alongside his escort boat, enduring cold water, jellyfish stings, and heavy seas, swimming for the French coastline. Night fell, and a dense fog rolled in. He couldn't see land, and with the fog and wind, he couldn't tell if he was even heading south toward France anymore. As he approached the second day, still swimming blind in the fog, his body gave out. As the escort crew hauled him aboard, the sun rose and the fog began to lift. Land came into view. They were a mere hundred yards from shore. Success was *right there*, but Webb had failed to see it.

Less than two weeks later, he was back at the Admiralty Pier in Dover, slathering oil on his bare skin and diving into the icy water for a second attempt. Currents repeatedly pushed him off course, forcing him to swim an extra forty miles, but twenty-two hours later, he touched ground in Calais, France. His feat made him famous.

NO TROPHIES IN DEFEAT

I tell that story to aspiring entrepreneurs who ask me about my own success in business. Many of them believe success comes suddenly—you have one brilliant idea and you get instantly rich—but I use the Matthew Webb story to explain that it doesn't work that way.

To succeed in any endeavor, you must be willing to push ahead and work through all the challenges, little and big, standing in your way. You have to fight through the fog that obscures your goal. You have to keep swimming when your arms are heavy. If you're going to get anywhere, you have to anticipate failure, overcome it, and learn from it the way Matthew Webb did.

There are always setbacks, complications, and disappointments. In fact, the closer you get to a breakthrough, whether it's in business or another pursuit, the harder the challenges get. This is when people often quit, and that's why there is such a high failure rate for businesses.

All too many aspiring entrepreneurs don't know where to begin. They are paralyzed by fear of failure, thinking, *What if I invest all my savings and the business fails? What if I quit my job to start this new venture and I wind up broke? What if I try out for that sports team and I get cut?*

Part of the problem is that our culture is built around instant gratification. It rewards us just for trying and doesn't prepare us for the hard knocks life dishes out. I first noticed this when my kids played Little League. When a player hit a ground ball and got thrown out at first base, he was allowed to stay on base anyway. At the end of the season, everyone got a participation trophy. It didn't matter whether the kids won or lost, or finished first or last. No one was allowed to fail.

Unfortunately, that's not how the real game is played. Why train hard or practice long hours if you'll get a trophy for finishing last? Why work on your hitting if you get to stay on base when you ground out? Disguising failure robs kids of life's lessons, and the result is that too many young people never develop the necessary resilience and incentive to improve.

People reach adulthood with an aversion to risk and a sense of entitlement. They expect job offers to flow into their inbox. They want high-paying internships. They fail to see the connection between success and hard work. They don't know how to brush off defeat and try again. They've learned that failure is a sign that they should stop what they're doing, move on, and play it safe. *It wasn't meant to be,* they think. *Oh well. I tried.*

The truth is that the marketplace doesn't reward failure. It rewards those who are unfazed by failure. Winners aren't defeated by their mistakes, they are strengthened by them. They examine failure, learn what caused it, and make adjustments so it doesn't happen again.

TROUBLE IS OPPORTUNITY

I grew up in rural Connecticut in a family with fewer resources than many of the people we knew. My father built our house, a project that took many years. We had plywood floors until I was in high school. My mom and I still joke about how we were always pulling slivers out of our feet.

I started working at a young age, mowing lawns and

painting houses. When I was fourteen, I lied about my age and got a job at a restaurant washing dishes at night. The restaurant was about five miles away, so I rode to work on a bike built out of spare parts. When I was older, I taught myself how to play drums and earned extra cash playing in rock bands.

After college, I started a real estate development company with my two older brothers. Eventually, we parted ways and at the age of forty-seven, I run the operation myself.

My company has built restaurants, public libraries, community centers, and sports complexes—the kind of projects where delays and disruptions are an everyday occurrence. Building materials aren't delivered on time. One subcontractor is late and throws off the entire schedule. The owners insist on one thing while the municipal planner requires something else. Even before the first brick is laid, you are at the mercy of local citizens showing up at a zoning hearing to complain about your project. There are so many people with their hands on so many different switches, that conflicts, obstacles, mistakes, and miscommunication are inevitable.

When you are a construction manager like me, everything that happens is your fault. If the project is late, the penalty comes out of your pocket, regardless of whose fault it was. This can be nerve-wracking, and there have been many times in my career when I couldn't sleep at night from worry. Even today, I still face moments of intense stress.

In spite of these setbacks, I've succeeded because I've learned to look at trouble as an opportunity—a time to learn, reflect, and develop new tactics. Each blow my company absorbs is another opportunity to prevail and get better, stronger, and more confident. It's the only way to grow.

THE PATH TO SUCCESS

My goal with this book is to help you think differently about your path to success. That path has stumbling blocks—obstacles, risks, and outright failure—not because of your mistakes or weaknesses, but because *that's the way it is with everybody*. From Matthew Webb to Sylvester Stallone to Oprah Winfrey, any successful person will acknowledge that their route to achievement and fame was perilous and slow moving. The only way they reached their goals was to *embrace their failure*, learn from it, and then get back to work.

The following chapters contain all the essential lessons I've learned along the way. These are the things I wish someone had told me when I was starting out.

Here are some of the topics we'll cover:

- **Chapter 1: Risk, Fear, Failure, Repeat.** Failure is normal, so we'll learn how to reprogram your mind to take advantage of setbacks.
- **Chapter 2: Two Mindsets.** If you're pessimistic and focused on protecting your assets, a scarcity mindset overwhelms the abundance mindset, which is required in order to see the great possibilities in life.
- **Chapter 3: Doing Nothing Is a Big Decision.** The status quo is dull and unrewarding, so find your dream and pursue it every day.
- **Chapter 4: The Enabler's Guide to Failure.** Enablers look for every excuse to avoid risks, and they don't want you to take chances. We'll talk about how to spot enablers and why you must avoid them.
- **Chapter 5: Charting Your Road map.** Overcoming anxiety about failure starts with developing strong habits and staying focused on your overarching goals. For most people, anxiety is just a rehearsal for being afraid. Stop rehearsing. I'll give you some tips that will help.
- **Chapter 6: The Real Truth about Personal and Business Finances.** The best way to deal with failure is to plan for it by being smart with your money.
- **Chapter 7: Entrepreneurship 101.** Whatever your business, certain things are required for success: integrity, strict accounting, and a willingness to fail.

Whether you are launching a new enterprise or pursuing a new career path, you need to leverage the power of failure to your advantage. You need to harness your fear. I'll give you the tools, practical strategies, and plenty of anecdotal evidence to teach you how to identify and overcome these problems to find success. Remember: your real enemy isn't failure or risk, but inertia.

It's normal to fear failure, but the biggest mistake you can make in business and in life is to be scared and do nothing about it. Instead, be ready to embrace failure and learn to turn it around, because it's your only route to success. When you learn to capitalize on your failures, your mindset shifts and the possibilities emerge like the sun rising through a fog.

Are you ready to take the plunge?

Chapter 1

RISK, FEAR, FAILURE, REPEAT

As I write this, football fans in Massachusetts and eastern Connecticut are celebrating because Tom Brady and the New England Patriots won Super Bowl LIII.

Everyone knows who Tom Brady is because he's a superstar quarterback and a future Hall of Famer who has won the Super Bowl six times, and has been the MVP of the NFL three times. He's a legend, and he makes winning look easy.

What people don't see, however, are all the setbacks Brady endured on his way to success. They forget that he wasn't drafted by the Patriots until the sixth round, or that he threw four interceptions in a game against his rival and former teammate Drew Bledsoe. They forget the knee injury in 2008 that kept him out of the game for a year and had many people saying his career was over.

Fans forget about all those Brady failures because he has a way of shrugging off defeat, learning from his mistakes, and throwing himself back into his work. He starts his workouts at 5:30 a.m., and when other teammates start showing up an hour later he greets them by saying, "Good afternoon!" He follows a strict diet. Considered slow most of his career, he worked on his speed and agility and became faster at age 39 than he was in college.

Brady has become a great quarterback by following a tried-and-true recipe for success. That recipe is what I call *risk, fear, failure, repeat.* To find success, you have to accept the risks, experience the fear, learn from failure, and then do it all over again. It's a process. Brady was fat and slow in high school and worked his way into the starting lineup. At the University of Michigan, he played behind six other quarterbacks before his hard work and preparation took him to the top. In the pros, he was a fourth-string quarterback before finally getting a chance to start. Throughout his career, Brady has had to continually prove himself, and he was always willing to put in the hours of practice needed to do that.

The difference between a winner and a loser is often minimal. What separates them is their attitude about failure. The loser fails and loses confidence. The winner fails and is inspired to get better—to get stronger, faster, and smarter. Winners use failure to build their confidence.

To reach excellence, whether it's in professional football or business, you must learn that fear and adversity are not your enemies. They are necessities in business and life. No one enjoys being afraid, but successful people understand that they can't grow and learn without fear. If you want good grades, a great job, or to start a successful business, you are going to have to go through fear first. You can either acknowledge that and keep moving forward, or you can turn around and run away.

You will fail, probably many times, before you succeed. For that reason, you can't treat risk, fear, and failure as a sign to quit. Instead, you have to think about it as a route to success.

FOLLOW THE RECIPE

The best way to learn the value of fear and failure is to follow a few general rules:

- **Acknowledge the fear.** When you decide to take a risk, whether it's starting a new business or asking someone out on a date, you have to admit that the idea scares you. There is no point in hiding your trepidation or pretending it doesn't exist.

- **Keep it in perspective.** You're scared of the challenge and worried about the outcome, but you have to acknowledge that there is nothing unusual about fear. Everyone knows fear. When you accept that fear and your efforts to overcome it are a recurring part of a rewarding life, you won't agonize so much over it.
- **Remember: you're going to be fine.** This is an essential attitude to have. When I was younger and building my business, I put a lot of pressure on myself and worried about many things. I wish someone had been around to reassure me that I'd get through it just fine. What I needed to hear was, "Don't freak out, Mat. All this shit's going to go wrong, but you're smart and hardworking, and the adversity will make you stronger and smarter. So relax. You'll be fine."
- **Laugh at it.** This is easier said than done, but try it out the next time you're going out on a limb and feeling fearful. *Oh boy. Look at how far I'll fall if I fuck this up. Hahahaha.* It's easier to laugh off a tense situation when you have faith in your abilities. Your fear is not a sign of weakness.
- **Have a plan.** Although this book will help you see the value of taking risks, I'm not advocating that you make reckless decisions just to see what happens. For significant challenges, develop multiple scenarios for overcoming them. If Plan A doesn't work, go to

Plan B. And don't settle for just having a Plan A and B. Develop Plans C and D, too, and use elements from them if the situation calls for it. Be ready to take corrective measures when you encounter any obstacles.

- **Make small adjustments over time.** Failures are not always enormous. Most of us face little failures or setbacks in the course of our daily lives. In situations like this, the key is to learn from these missteps and make adjustments along the way.

Here's the point: the risk-fear-failure-repeat cycle is a pattern you will see over and over again in your life. Get used to it. You are going face risk, feel fear, and fall down from time to time. When you pick yourself up, you must review what went wrong, understand how to avoid the same stumble in the future, and then move forward, ready to go through it all again. Your failures are not bad luck or lousy karma. These failures occurred because you *tried something* instead of running away. This is the road to success.

BUILDING CONFIDENCE

The best way to capitalize on risk, fear, failure, repeat is to build your confidence. I know that sounds like a paradox. How do you gain confidence from failing? Nothing can break your confidence like a dose of failure, right?

True. But failure exposes a hole in your vision or knowledge, so when you acknowledge your missteps, review what caused them, and make a plan for dealing with them in the future, you plug those holes. You come away from the experience smarter and more experienced. And *that* process breeds confidence.

I compare the process to going to the gym. When you work out, you are engaging in controlled failure. You are bench pressing until you can't anymore, or you are running until your lungs burn and your legs are rubber. You are pushing your body until it fails.

Why do you do that? You do that because you believe in the training effect. You know that if you stress your body and then give it a chance to recover, it will come back stronger than before. In your next workout you'll be able to do more than last time, and this allows you to continually improve. Over time, you become bigger and faster—and more confident. You trust the process and trust your body's ability to snap back.

This same attitude helps you through the risk-fear-failure-repeat process.

Seventy-five percent to 90 percent of doctor visits in the United States are the result of people suffering from stress. Yet many people come away from anxious times with what researchers call "greater mental fortitude."

Stress can help people improve their memory, problem-solving skills, and analytical abilities.

It's all in how you perceive the risk, fear, and failure. Here are the key elements of a healthy perspective:

- **Maintain control.** You are the captain of your own ship. You decide when to trim the sails and when to jibe. You determine just how much wind you and your boat can handle. People who maintain control over their lives tend to look at stress as a form of exhilaration, just like when your sails fill and your craft heels, and you have to lean far out over the water. It's wild and rousing, but you're not afraid, because you're in charge.
- **Keep moving.** In other words, keep working and learning. Those who have grit and determination have a more active left brain hemisphere (the reward-seeking region), and that prevents the anxious right hemisphere from taking over.
- **State your values.** Take a moment to jot down your personal values. What does it mean to you to be a good human, and how are you measuring up to your own values? Keep this document handy and revisit it from time to time to record your ongoing efforts to be a better person.
- **Reassess.** People who occasionally re-examine their lives are better able to handle stress. There is nothing

new about this idea—Socrates said that the unexamined life is not worth living—but I think a lot of people don't take the time to practice this valuable insight. So occasionally take several steps back from your life and examine what has shaped you and how you've used this knowledge to improve as a person. What have you learned in the last six months? What are you going to do differently in light of that knowledge?

· **Don't take it personally.** You can't think of your failure as a personal attack. Our emotional response to problems is often not based on logic, so if you can think about a setback in a dispassionate way, you redirect your thoughts away from the emotional centers of the brain—the parts of the brain that produce fear and anger—and into the problem-solving frontal lobes.

· **Recalibrate and reinvent.** People who are the most resilient in stressful situations tend to be those who can quickly adapt to new circumstances and focus on the path forward. Acknowledge your strengths, but also your limitations, as you figure out what to do next. Ask yourself, *Have my goals for the future changed?* If so, is the path you're on still the right one?

If you have this kind of healthy perspective, fear and anxiety become positive forces. When your hands are a little shaky, your palms are sweaty, and your heart is beating faster than normal, your brain and body know that these symptoms will pass. This helps you build a stronger, more confident attitude that enables you to face future problems.

I look at this as a process of building mental strength. I'm not suggesting a personality overhaul, but rather micro-adjustments of attitude that lead to greater success.

Baseball is an excellent example of this process. In baseball, the player who hits .275 is good, and the player who hits .300 is great. When a player only hits .250, the coaches say the player "lacks confidence." But with small improvements—a more open stance, say, or better hip movement—and lots of practice, a .250 hitter can get up to .280 or even .300. The batters who see their weaknesses and work to overcome them gain confidence, perform better, and learn to handle more challenging situations.

The same risk-fear-failure-repeat process of diligent self-improvement and dispassionate problem solving applies before you even start your business. There's a lot you don't know when you're starting out. Embrace it and get to work building your knowledge and minimizing your weaknesses. As you become more experienced and build on what you know, you'll be increasingly more equipped to deal with whatever comes your way.

DIAMONDS FROM LUMPS OF COAL

As I mentioned in the introduction, I grew up in modest circumstances. I could see that other families had more than us, and I made a decision that I didn't want to remain poor.

People who come up from severe hardship tend to go one of two paths: one that leads to a life of crime and drugs, or a path of hard work that leads to success. People like Oprah Winfrey and Sylvester Stallone overcame the grim circumstances of their early years because of a strong desire and willingness to work hard.

Oprah's teenaged mother left her with relatives in Mississippi when Oprah was still a baby, and as a young girl, Oprah bounced around among relatives' houses in Mississippi, Milwaukee, and Nashville. She had to grow up fast, and television was often her only companion. Before she was ten, Oprah was already dreaming of someday being a TV star herself. She learned to read and write early, and became comfortable in front of audiences by speaking regularly to her church congregation.

Stallone, meanwhile, grew up on the mean streets of New York City. He spent some early years in foster care and was expelled from high school before finally catching on as an actor in New York. But even that was not easy for him, and he didn't make it big until he wrote the screenplay for *Rocky*.

Both of these performers developed the mental strength and resilience needed to handle the stress of their early lives.

While I didn't go on to star in any movies, my own experience early in life was similar. I was determined to follow a path that would take me from the dire straits and financial stress of my youth to a successful career. Along the way I learned to deal with stress and risk in beneficial ways.

When some people hear of the financial risks I take in real estate and construction, they tell me that they can't imagine how I deal with it. They'll say, "You just took out a loan for *how much*? Are you nuts? How do you handle the stress?"

What they don't understand is that stress is part of the job. For me, that short-term financing is a measure of the challenge in front of me. It means I've got skin in the game and potential for success in the construction project I'm undertaking. In order to succeed, I learned the recipe of risk, fear, failure, and repeat. It's the secret sauce that got me to this place.

Remember: A diamond is just a lump of coal that's been subjected to tremendous pressure over a long period of time. Good things come from learning to deal with the pressures and stresses of living.

YOUR TWENTY-MINUTE PLAN

It's important for young entrepreneurs to understand that failure is not the scary proposition many people make it out to be. You should not make decisions based on a desire to avoid failure. Trial and error are not a sign of failure, but a measure of your stubborn ambition—something you need to make it big in business. The more new things you attempt, the more you fail and the more you learn. That knowledge and experience makes you stronger and more confident. This is how experience is developed.

It's critical to have a goal for where you want to go. I call it a rallying cry. This is your private clarion call, the phrase you use to remember your deepest intentions. This is your why. Whether you are starting a new business or a new career, you must have a central mission, and you must be prepared to overcome a lot of obstacles to get there.

Once you have your objective, draw a map to get there. By map, I don't mean simple directions. It's much more than that. Your map has to include the steps you'll take, of course, but it must also include the people or tools you need, the knowledge gaps you'll have to fill, and the manner in which you will pursue your objective. What relationships do you need to cultivate? How will you dress? Can you be your regular, earthy self or will you need to break out the shoe polish and Brylcreem?

For example, when we expanded my company, it was important to me that we continued to operate with a strong moral belief system. Regardless of what type of project it is, all of our decisions are focused on one question: what's best for the customer? People in the construction business often have a terrible reputation, and some of that is deserved, but I was determined that we would rise above that and be different. We would be as good as our word. We would make our deadlines. We would admit our mistakes if we made them, and we would make amends. In everything we do, we want to be fair, honest, and transparent.

Anyone thinking about becoming an entrepreneur must also reach that point. You must give long, hard thought to what kind of character you want your company to have and what lengths you're willing to go to establish and maintain that character. I don't mean you have to be stiff and formal—although that might be the best choice for you—but whatever it is, your personality must shine through and appeal to people, or your business or career won't be sustainable.

Some of what I'm suggesting may sound daunting, but I encourage you to take the time and do it right. I advise people facing significant projects or big challenges like this to break things down to their smallest common denominators. This is the best way to measure forward progress. The experts talk about how you need a one-year, ten-year, or twenty-year plan. But the size of those goals can be intimidating and discouraging. It can feel like you're not getting any closer to where you want to be.

So I recommend people have a twenty-minute plan. Ask yourself, *What am I going to do for the next twenty minutes to get closer to my goal?* You have a small job to accomplish, so focus on it with all you've got. As you get better at these twenty-minute clips, they'll start to add up. Each one follows the last, rolling out in front of you and making steady progress.

THE BIG THREE

You may still encounter distractions and setbacks, so I also recommend what I call "The Big Three." It's a technique I use with my sons. It started out as a sarcastic, wise-ass concept I would say to them when they did something incredibly stupid. Then it started to have real-world applications to a great many people. Go figure.

Here are The Big Three questions:

1. What am I doing right now?
2. Where am I going?
3. What is going on around me?

For my kids, it's a way to keep their wits about them. For people contemplating careers in business, it's a strategy for clearing away distractions and reassessing where you stand in relation to your goals in real time. Once you nail down The Big Three questions, you can refocus on the task at hand, knowing it fits your overarching goal.

The Big Three has worked very well in my job. When you're managing a construction project, things can get hectic and complicated. You're multitasking all day long. You're on the phone, sending emails and texts, talking with clients and subcontractors, solving problems, and scheduling work. It can feel overwhelming.

At those times, I take a deep breath and go through The Big Three. What's the biggest priority at that moment? What's the thing that's going to blow my boat out of the water? Okay, let's tackle that one first, then move on to the next one. We have outstanding project management software in our office, but The Big Three is very effective for thinking through my main tasks of the day. I write them down, get them done, and check them off. As I always say, if you want something done, make a list.

TRUE MEASURE OF SUCCESS

It's crucial that your central goals focus on more than personal wealth and success. If you follow the risk-fear-failure-repeat cycle and become strong and confident, your ultimate success must be more than significant income and driving wicked-nice cars. Take it from me: I've owned some really nice cars, and I've learned that they are not important. They are not a measure of your success.

The true measure of your success is how much you help other people. I want you to be successful, but in the end, there is much more to life than big houses and vacations to the Caribbean. This world needs a generation of young people who are selfless and prepared to do great things to help others.

The greatest innovators in our world today are not the ruthless "greed is good" Gordon Gekko characters we see in movies like *Wall Street*. Instead, they are generous, humble, and curious. They don't pretend to have all the answers themselves, but understand that solutions come from many sources and people. The best way to access those sources and people is through kindness and good intentions, not greed and power.

And, as we'll learn in the next chapter, it also takes a certain kind of mindset.

Chapter 2

THE TWO MINDSETS

My paternal grandparents lived through the Great Depression, the worst economic downturn in our country's history. Middle-class families were forced to stand in line for food, and children dropped out of school to work and earn something for the family. People like my grandfather Pepe found it difficult or impossible to be the breadwinners in their families, and they lost the sense of purpose and pride that came from providing for their loved ones. It was a brutal, often humiliating time, and it instilled in my grandparents the importance of being cautious and frugal. They grew their own food, passed down clothing from generation to generation, and lived in a way designed to preserve what they had.

The Great Depression ended in the late 1930s, and our country recovered and entered a period of prosperity after World War II. We've had economic booms and some scary busts since then (remember the Great Recession of 2008?). But for the most part, things have never again gotten as desperate as they were in the 1930s when there were no safety nets for people who struggled, no government entitlement programs to fall back on, no reassurance that they could still put food on the table when their kids were hungry.

Despite economic improvements since my grandfather's time, many people today have a *scarcity mindset*. They live in fear of losing a job, or getting socked with a big car repair bill, or losing their home in a natural disaster or a new financial crisis. As a result, they don't take risks. They don't test themselves. They aren't willing to try something new, or even to contemplate trying something different.

On the other side of the coin are people with an *abundance mindset*. Those with an abundance mindset are not satisfied with what they have. They enjoy the pleasures of life, but at the same time they dream of earning more, accomplishing more, and helping more. It's not always about money. People with an abundance mindset want to get better grades, grow a more significant business, get promotions and better jobs, or work to get better at a sport. The abundance mindset sees the possibilities in the world and sees no reason not to reach out and grab those opportunities, even if it involves risk.

These two types of people don't understand each other. If you put people with an abundance mindset in the same room with people with a scarcity mindset, they would express very different points of view. One side thinks, *Why would you take that kind of risk?* The other side thinks, *Why are these people so afraid of trying something new?* When we were kids, my brothers and I used to joke about our grandparents and how they could never part with a buck. We didn't understand their point of view. This is not to criticize them or other people who went through what they went through, but it does explain how difficult it is for those with a sense of abundance to understand those with a fear of scarcity.

ARE YOU THRILLED OR PUT OFF BY NEW CHALLENGES?

To succeed in life, whether you are starting your own business or a new career, it's imperative that you have an abundance mindset. You must have ambitious goals and a desire to tackle any question that stands in your way. You have to anticipate changes and embrace new challenges, or you will find your customers have moved on to do business with your more progressive competitor. This is not to say people with an abundance mindset have short attention spans and are always racing off to try the latest innovation. What I mean is that those with a sense of abundance are thrilled to tackle new challenges in the name of prosperity, knowledge, and personal success—

whether that comes in the form of greater income or in the form of greater social good.

Those with a scarcity mindset merely want a job with a paycheck. They want to be able to pay their bills and maybe save a little. They are looking for any port in a storm because every day brings threatening clouds to their horizon.

Those with a scarcity mindset even look at victory, emotions, and relationships differently than those with an abundance mindset. Scarcity-minded people look at success as a victory over someone, and they have a hard time expressing genuine glee for the achievements of their friends, colleagues, and family members. They aren't particularly good on teams because they don't share credit, and see disagreements as disloyalty. Their abundant counterparts, meanwhile, think success occurs when everybody wins. They like collaborating, and they are drawn to the idea of changing and improving and trying new things.

In fairness, scarcity is sometimes a good thing. For instance, right now I'm writing this book and my editor wants this draft completed in three days. Three days! That's not enough time! But it's that very scarcity of time that will make today and the next two days so memorable for me. I will be getting more out of every waking moment because I will be intensely focused on this book and these ideas. Distractions will be less tempting and my sense of mission will be heightened. In this state, new connections will materialize, new possibilities will surface.

I'm looking forward to this stripped-down process. When I'm done, I will feel very satisfied (I just hope my editor will be, too).

Scarcity also heightens our sense of the value of things, and that is also good. My grandparents treasured things that many of us today might think of as insignificant— an old car that still runs, a comfortable Oxford shirt that gets hand-washed because my grandfather loves the feel of the fabric against his skin. When you go without long enough, little things take on bigger dimensions.

Scarcity should not be confused with desperation. Sometimes great accomplishments and brilliant ideas come out of desperation. When your back is against the wall and you have "burned the boats," it's do or die. Unfortunately, many die. But some rise to the occasion and excellence is born.

The scarcity mindset I see most often today is not helpful to young people contemplating how to make their mark on the economy or life. The scarcity mindset I see is an impoverished mentality where people are too focused on the present and on their immediate surroundings. They are not looking expansively into the future. They are content to sit on the couch playing *Fortnite* instead of going out the door for a run through the neighborhood. They squander their time on little things and give scant attention to larger investments that can pay off down the road. You may think you are too busy to take that business class two nights a week. Are you? How might that business class pay off down the road? Someone with an abundance mindset would see the possibilities immediately and set aside household chores so they have time for the class.

People with a scarcity mindset too often settle for a safe job with a steady paycheck. They just go to work and do what the boss tells them to do. But is that kind of scarcity mindset really safe? What happens if the company falls on hard times and has to fire you? When you look at it this way, a scarcity mindset is a more dangerous way of living. You are relying on someone else to provide for you, and that attitude offers a false sense of security.

This is not to say that people with a scarcity mindset are weak or miserable. There are wonderful people in this world—my grandparents included—who lived with a scarcity mindset. But if you want more out of life—more satisfaction and more impact on the world—then adopting an abundance mindset is imperative.

Reading this, you might have identified yourself as having a scarcity mindset. That's okay. It's not like you're condemned now to a life of indecision and worry. Instead, you can now look at your fear and inertia in a different light.

See it for what it is—something holding you back—and do something about it. Set some big goals, but chunk those projects into smaller pieces that you can tackle one at a time. For example, you're not going to quit smoking, lose weight, and run a marathon all in six months. So set some interim goals. Quit smoking first and start taking walks. Add some jogging to your walks after a while. Cut back on the cookies and ice cream at night and start tracking your weight. Concentrating on a few achievable goals at a time increases your odds of overall success. None of these activities requires that constricting sense of fear or doom that often hangs over the mind of someone with a scarcity mindset, and your successes will add up and give you the confidence to look farther into the future. We'll talk more in chapter five about setting goals, but for now, be assured that there is a way out of the angst you feel about the future.

The solution is taking action.

THE STOCK MARKET METAPHOR

A great way to discern the difference between a scarcity

mindset and an abundance mindset is by examining how people operate in and view the stock market. Frightened people with a scarcity mindset are hardwired to make poor choices when it comes to investing, while those who are more calm and self-assured do extremely well.

For example, in the last few weeks, the stock market has taken a pummeling. There's been a 20 percent decline, and though this is a significant drop, it's not that unusual. The stock market always goes through ups and downs, but people with different mindsets view those fluctuations differently.

When the stock market plummets 20 percent, all the people with scarcity mindsets freak out and sell their holdings. They see their money dwindling and they can't tolerate the fear of further losses. They pull out of the stock market, take a huge loss, and stuff their cash into their mattress. They sit down and stare at their trembling hands and ask themselves why they took that risk in the first place. Never again!

Thanks to this sell-off by the fainthearted, stocks go down even farther.

When people with an abundance mindset see this happening, they smile and start buying stocks at bargain basement prices. They are happy to take the cheap stocks offered by scarcity-minded investors. Later, when those scarcity people see stock prices going back up, they start buying again, thinking it's safe.

When that happens, those with the abundance mindset win. It happens every time. Those who invested when everyone else was running for their lives benefit as stock prices climb and those bargain-basement stocks grow and grow in value. The brave ones make a 20 percent profit while the timid folks lose. This process has been happening for a hundred years, and it's going to continue. One side is trying to preserve themselves so they can live another day, while the other side is taking the longer view: *I'm going to let you guys run for the hills like scared rabbits. Let the stock market dip and fluctuate, or crash. As soon as prices hit bottom and there are dead bodies everywhere, I'm going to buy.*

An investor like Warren Buffett has an abundance mindset. He believes the market will inherently go up again because that is what it's done over the last century. Buffett is old, boring, and patient, and you won't hear about how much he's made until after the market recovers. If you're looking for an instant profit, then investing is dangerous. But if you take the long view and you have integrity, confidence, and faith in mankind, like Warren Buffett does, you can make a ton of money buying when everyone else is selling. When everyone else is running for the exits, you're walking against the flow of people to get inside. When you have an abundance mindset, you buy when everything is on sale. That is where great wealth happens.

This principle of abundance applies in business as well as the stock market. In the real estate development business that I'm in, we can't afford to buy assets when the market is booming. Prices are just too high, and we can't turn a profit. I see our competitors buying and I ask them, "How the hell do you guys turn a profit?" and they tell me, "Oh, prices are going to keep going up." Are they? Really? No, they aren't. This market is going to crash, and that's when we'll buy.

CHANGING YOUR MINDSET

The first step in changing your scarcity mindset is to acknowledge who you are and decide that you want to change. I compare it to the time twenty years ago when I decided to quit smoking. Smoking is clearly stupid, but back then it was widely accepted. Still, that's not an excuse. The first thing I did was to admit that I was addicted. The second step was making the commitment to quit. I had to decide that I didn't want anything to have control over me anymore.

Those who want to change their scarcity mindset have to do the same thing. As I mentioned, you may have to break your goals down into doable chunks, but you also have to keep your oars in the water. You have to keep rowing, put your back into it, and look for better opportunities. One of the hardest challenges will be changing how you view the ideas of others. You can't think of those ideas as a threat, or the people as a threat. Don't worry so much about personal success as you do about the success of the group. Remember the adage: there are three ways to do things—my way, your way, and a better way.

This notion of abundance goes beyond wealth. That's part of it, of course, but embracing the idea of abundance means you want to experience more. You want to help more people. You want to have a greater impact on your family and your community. You have to acknowledge that you're tired of worrying about your car breaking down and reassure yourself that if it does break down, you'll find a way to fix it or get a new one. If you decide to buy a new car, donate your old one to the humane society so they can help animals. That's abundance.

Again, confidence is a crucial element to an abundance mindset. To see the possibilities in life, you need self-reliance and faith that you'll be able to figure out answers when the tough questions are blocking your path. Here are some ways to do that.

STAY ON YOUR PATH

If you're an entrepreneur starting a business, you probably already have an abundance mindset. That's excellent. But you still need to keep working on your idea, regardless of the failures or setbacks you encounter. Just because you're optimistic about your future doesn't mean you don't have to work hard and swim against the tide from time to time.

TALK ABOUT THE OBSTACLES YOU'LL FACE

Having an abundance mindset doesn't mean you blithely glide over every hurdle. You won't. Instead, you have to anticipate potential problems and start plotting how you'll get past them. If you're confident and optimistic, the answers come more quickly and in greater numbers, thus improving your chances of success. You can't assume your business idea is going to be a mega-hit right from the start, and that you'll make tons of money. That might happen, but chances are you'll have to work some long, hard hours first.

DEVELOP GOOD HABITS

We'll talk more about this in chapter five, but for now, it's vital that you set strong goals and adopt the habits that will help you reach those goals. Networking is key to learning and to building contacts and community. It's not just about the help you can receive, but the help you can give. Find ways to appreciate the uniqueness of others, whether you're working with them or having a cocktail at the local pub.

ADDRESS ONE PROBLEM AT A TIME

Starting a new business is often daunting. You may have a dream of what you want to accomplish, but the task in front of you seems overwhelming. Where do you start?

I like the approach Desmond Tutu once advocated. "There is only one way to eat an elephant," he said. "One bite at a time." What this means is that the bigger the endeavor, the more crucial it is that you break up the challenge into smaller pieces. The problems seem less intimidating and more doable when you look at them in smaller, discrete portions.

It's not unusual for people to freeze up or get discouraged when faced with a big, hairy task, so in addition to the wisdom of Desmond Tutu, it also helps to keep in mind this observation by Mark Twain: "The secret to getting ahead is getting started." It's much easier to make progress in your big goal when you chip away at the challenges.

DON'T KICK THE CAN

It may be tempting to put off work on a particularly gnarly

problem or to delay a decision on something until you have more information, but be forewarned: you can only kick the can down the road so many times before it becomes the size of a fifty-gallon drum. When that happens, procrastination is no longer an option.

Instead, just make a decision. Whether it's the right decision or the wrong one, at least *you did something*. If it turns out to be the wrong decision, at least now you know what *not* to do, and you're halfway there. You'll learn and you'll be able to adjust. You miss those opportunities when you put off making a move. Wayne Gretzky once pointed out that you will miss 100 percent of the shots you never take.

SETTING YOUR GOALS

One critical way to shift your mindset from scarcity to abundance is to determine your goals and write them down. People who have a vivid picture of their goals are twice as likely to accomplish those goals.

Write them down in detail and post them in a conspicuous place—the door of your refrigerator or on the whiteboard in your office—to keep your mission front and center. It's a regular reminder. The act of writing down goals also helps ensure they are embedded in your mind.

Writing down your goals gives them prominence and

makes them more of a priority. That's why many companies today have vision boards where they can openly and creatively display their goals and mission. It's a way of keeping your priorities at the top of your mind, and helps you stay accountable.

I have a business coach, and the first thing he has me do at the beginning of each year is write down my goals. At first, I thought this was a little childish, but he was adamant, and now it's an annual ritual. My coach is a successful, experienced businessman, and what he's doing is holding me accountable. We review those goals from time to time during the year, so I'm always aware of how much (or how little) progress I've made, so I can adjust my efforts as necessary.

Having goals in writing also clears up any confusion. If you merely *say* what your goals are, they aren't as fixed and definite. When they are written down, you can't trick yourself into conveniently forgetting or being imprecise about what you remember.

GETTING SMART

The best goals are those that are Specific, Measurable, Attainable, Relevant, and Timely. Your chance of attaining goals increases when they have these qualities. Here's what each characteristic means:

SPECIFIC

Your goal needs to be as unambiguous as possible. For instance, rather than saying one of your goals is to "turn a profit in the first year" of your new business, you might say, "achieve a 10 percent profit margin" in that first year. Try to imagine what your life will be like if you achieve this goal, and that will ensure you stay motivated throughout the year as you measure your profit.

MEASURABLE

Make sure you can measure progress toward your goal. After all, you want to be able to know when it's time to celebrate, right? Again, this is where Desmond Tutu's advice comes in handy: create a series of smaller goals that contribute to an overall goal (one bite at a time). If you're starting a business, set up goals for each step: 1) create a business name, 2) get all the necessary licenses you need to get started, 3) set up a reliable accounting system, and so forth. It's easier to stay on track toward that big goal when you can successfully complete each smaller goal that supports that overarching end goal. It's like gaining yardage on each down in a football game.

ATTAINABLE

Be realistic. Don't make your goal too ambitious or you

run the risk of failing and getting discouraged. Selling snowplows in Jamaica is a shitty idea and a bad goal.

RELEVANT

Make sure your goal is important to you. If the target doesn't excite you, you're less likely to work on it, particularly when the going gets tough.

TIMELY

Each goal you set must have a deadline. Only then will you remain committed to achieving it. Targets that have no timetable are too easy to set aside, but looming deadlines will keep you on task.

It's also wise to have personal goals, as well as business goals. For example, I recently made it a personal goal to work less in the coming year. When I mentioned this, my business coach held my feet to the fire: specifically how much less do you want to work? Since I've been working up to seventy hours a week for the last twenty years, I made it my goal to drop down to forty hours a week. I also made it my goal to take a vacation this year—something I haven't done in several years.

I wrote down these goals and posted them in my office the same way I do with my professional goals. In this way, they are just as important and imperative to me. Now I am reminded of those goals and can measure my progress. How am I doing on cutting down my hours? Do I need to delegate more of my responsibilities to staff? What other steps can I take to reach my personal goals?

It helps to review your goals and your progress toward them every week. Do it at the beginning of the week so that you have the next three or four days to take specific steps toward achieving your goal. At the end of the week, look back and assess your progress. Ask yourself, *Do I need to pick up the pace to reach my goal by the appointed time?*

Again, break the goal down into discrete pieces. If your goal is to make $2 million in revenue for the year, divide $2 million by twelve and assess your progress each month. What do you have to do to hit your goal for this month? Where are you falling behind and where do you need to step up your game? Looking incrementally at your progress toward overarching goals can make your head explode, but breaking goals down and measuring progress keeps the process manageable and rewarding.

ABUNDANCE AND YOUR WORK RELATIONSHIPS

I've learned over the years that not only do you need to have an abundance mindset, but you need to work with people who also have an abundance mindset.

Earlier in my career, my company would hire subcontractors based on the bids for the work we needed. What I found, though, was that the lowest bidders were the ones with the scarcest mindset. They come in with great pricing, but when the work started, they would make one excuse after another for why they needed to be paid more. They start out talking a good game—"Oh, don't worry. We'll cover this, that, and the other thing"—then they start negotiating for more money.

Subcontractors with an abundance mindset are much easier to work with. They want to be part of your team and want to do right by the customer. If it takes more time and money to do the job right and meet their obligations, they accept it, because they want future jobs. They want to continue working with you. They see opportunities in working with you, and they want to be on a team that shares credit and recognition.

No matter what business you're going into, you'll eventually have to interact with other businesses. If those people have an abundance mindset like you, you're more likely to succeed. An abundance mindset gives you a bigger, fuller future with more potential, more possibilities. You want to work with people who feel the same way. A scarcity mindset only gives you a narrow, dark future, where you feel like you're just barely eking out a living.

EMPLOYEES WITH A SENSE OF ABUNDANCE

I also look for abundance mindsets when I'm hiring employees. While you might not mind if your accountant has a scarcity mindset, you certainly want your other employees to be energized, ambitious, and confident. You want to hire people who aren't afraid to take some chances and are willing to learn from their mistakes. They want to fit in, shine, and find ways to make your team better.

On the other hand, you want to avoid those scarcity mindset individuals who are afraid to make decisions and change course on a dime. You don't want anyone who's nervous, secretive, negative, or scared to death of losing their job. You want people who are excited to come in to work, not people who dread it. Some employers want their employees to fear being fired, but I don't think that kind of attitude contributes to the sense of abundance that I like to foster in my business. When people are continually looking over their shoulder expecting a pink slip, they are not inspired to do amazing things. But if they work for a boss who encourages them, they'll do work that inspires their boss. If they come to work saying, "I can't wait to kick ass today. Let's try out this improvement I've been thinking about," that's where innovation occurs.

THE VALUE OF GENEROSITY

We talked in the last chapter about how the measure of your success should be more than material wealth. It's nice to have quality possessions—a luxury car, a beautiful house—but the most successful innovators aim higher and reach for more profound results. They want to change the world. They want to genuinely help people with their products or services and contribute to causes like finding cures for cancer or solving homelessness or ending hunger. To reach those loftier goals requires much more than the relentless, take-no-prisoners approach to business that we associate with driven individuals like Steve Jobs.

Successful people, whether they are entrepreneurs or engineers, can pull together diverse ideas from different fields to find solutions to significant problems. They don't pretend to have all the answers themselves, but instead have a humble curiosity and an ability to bring divergent ideas together to find answers.

People who succeed at this level are generally friendly and humble. They make connections, volunteer, and pursue their natural inquisitiveness. Nobel Prize-winning physicist Richard Feynman, for instance, once showed up at the lab of a grad student studying artificial intelligence. Feynman performed all kinds of mundane tasks, from buying office supplies to soldering circuit boards. He was there to help and learn.

When you have an abundance mindset, you remember to share your success and the abundance that comes with it. It means putting your shoulder to the wheel, giving to worthy causes, volunteering, networking, and building relationships for the good of your community. It can be as simple as sponsoring a local soccer or baseball team. That's the kind of generosity that comes back to you ten times over.

Chapter 3

DOING NOTHING IS A BIG DECISION

My company started out focused on residential subdivision construction and we did very well in that area. Some of the jobs were small, but they grew and became more significant over time.

After a while, I felt we were painting ourselves with a very narrow brush and that we needed to broaden and diversify. It's true that we did excellent work in residential construction and had great success. But how long would that last? The residential market is notoriously cyclical: housing prices fluctuate, jobs come and go, and the market is dramatically influenced by dozens of factors outside our control. I wondered how long it would remain stable, and I wondered how many opportunities we were missing by focusing on building houses.

My company was at a crossroads, and we needed to decide whether to stay the course or expand into a new area. This is a common dilemma for entrepreneurs, but it's also a common personal question that individuals face. Should I start a new business? Should I abandon one career for another that offers more opportunities? Should I ask this person I love to marry me?

These are tough questions made more complicated by the risk involved. What if the business fails? What if I get laid off from my new job? What if marriage ruins a perfectly good relationship? Regardless of the scenario, the central question is: Why should I make changes when what I'm doing has paid off so well for me? Maybe I should just do what the British government told its citizens to do during World War II—"Keep calm and carry on."

Well, as a "ready, fire, and aim" kind of guy, you can imagine what I decided. We would not merely "carry on." Instead, my company branched out and diversified. In addition to residential construction, we took on more commercial construction management projects, which were often far more complex and risky than the type of work we were doing. We took on some jobs that were out of state. We moved out of our comfort zone and developed new skills, new connections, and an improved reputation. We weighed the risk of expanding, as well as the risk of standing pat, and decided that standing pat was riskier than expanding. Over time—and with a lot of hard work—it all paid off.

The process taught me a lot about the dangers of procrastinating and overanalyzing. People put off difficult decisions for many reasons—they're afraid of being wrong, they worry about failing, or they just don't know how to get started. So, instead of making a decision, they mull it over, run numbers, make lists of pros and cons, and basically just piddle around until the decision is made for them, or the opportunity disappears. In contrast, I weighed my company's options and took the plunge.

That's not to say we were reckless. Before we expanded, we asked ourselves a few simple questions:

- Is this the kind of work we love to do?
- Is this work sustainable? If we develop the capacity and knowledge to succeed in this new arena, will there be more opportunities in the future?
- Who will we be working with? Are they honest and forthright people?
- What are the risks if we fail?
- What are the risks if we stand pat?

DANGERS OF DOING NOTHING

People often don't consider the risk of standing pat

when they contemplate a new business or career. That's because many people don't consider the status quo to be risky. To them, the status quo feels pretty safe when they compare it to the unknown. Their brain perceives the risk and the unknown as potential pain or harm, and the resulting apprehension is often enough to throttle a person's ability to try something new.

However, doing nothing is often riskier than taking action. If you do nothing, how do you expect anything in your life or your business to change? I honestly believe that when I am sitting still doing nothing, I am wasting my life and my God-given skills, and I can't stand that.

Good entrepreneurs are always re-examining their professional strategies and looking for soft spots. They ask themselves, *Who are my customers and how have their needs or desires changed?* If their customers haven't changed, they start to look at their competitors. *What are they doing that we aren't doing?* Have your competitors introduced a skill or an approach you should also adopt? Throughout this process, good entrepreneurs are reading, sifting through societal, political, regulatory, or technological patterns that might reveal new opportunities or suggest a change.

Some of us are fortunate in that we have a lot of autonomy over our own business, but many of you are going to have partners or other team members who may not want to move as quickly and decisively as you. They always ask for more information or raise new questions with the primary goal of putting off a difficult decision. They are stalling.

Some people think they can't make a decision until they have so much data that the answer is obvious. But business often requires fast decisions based on incomplete information, so when you're working with partners, find out early in the process how much information your partners will need in order to make a move. What will it take for them to be confident enough to make a change to the business? This sends a message that you can't wait for easy answers and that your partners, if they want to work with you, will sometimes have to make decisions based on incomplete information.

THE DANGERS OF STAGNATION

When you or your company stays locked in the status quo, your perceived value declines. People don't expect much more from you than what you've done in the past. When I expanded my business, clients started looking at us differently. They could see we were ambitious and capable of doing more than building houses, and this opened up new opportunities for us, and our status grew.

The business world is full of examples of successful companies that take risks. Google has the foremost search engine on the planet, yet it is continually branching out into new fields. What do self-driving cars have to do with online search? Not much. But Google is focused on the future, and if self-driving cars are going to be a big part of the future, Google wants to be at the forefront.

Taking on new risks and challenges can help you become more insightful and decisive. Procrastinators are afraid to make decisions, so they never get good at making them. But those who take risks are often forced to make decisions, and they find that decision-making gets easier the more you do it. Risks become mere problems to address, not frightening roadblocks.

Starting and expanding your own business also gets easier. If you're working for a big company right now and sitting in a cubicle waiting for your next paycheck, you may feel safer than that high school buddy of yours starting an online store. But you have no control over your future.

However, if you're an entrepreneur and you're out there grinding and learning and making connections with clients and other businesses, you have all the control. You're not restricted to a cubicle, but instead are free to use your courage, experience, and relationships to try new and different things.

I used to think that the only people in this world who might be content with the status quo were old people— retirees who've worked hard all their lives and now want to kick back and enjoy the fruits of their labor. Then I met this guy who answered an ad of ours for an estimator. We were expanding and we'd enlisted all kinds of people to do estimates for us on projects we were bidding. These estimators all sucked. We were missing a lot of opportunities. We needed quick-moving people who had a lot of experience, and no one was filling the bill.

Then this guy called. On the phone, he sounded like he was forty years old. He'd worked for some huge construc-tion firms up and down the East Coast, and his references raved about him: "sharp as a razor," "knows all the soft-ware," "makes his deadlines," "does impeccable work." I thought to myself, *This is our guy.*

It turned out that he was seventy-nine years old. I was amazed.

You might think that a nearly eighty-year-old guy who'd had a great career would be happy with the status quo. People his age are retired and doing nothing, right? Wrong. This guy wasn't standing pat. He wanted new and different work, and he wanted to keep learning, keep moving forward. He was interested in expanding his business and finding new problems to solve. Well, so were we, so without hesitation I hired him.

THE NATURE OF RISK

Any time you own a business, you face some level of risk. You risk losing a key employee. You risk losing customers to a competitor. Your costs skyrocket at a time that your revenue drops. Your product's value plummets due to unforeseen market forces. Your distribution channel disappears. No matter how well you analyze your situation, risks are always lurking in the shadows.

The only thing you can do is to keep your eyes open and respond when trouble arises. Reach out to your customers. Diversify and find work in different but related fields. If business were predictable and risk free, everyone would do it, and the rewards would be insignificant. But the world of business is often capricious, and the only way to prepare for it is to develop a talent for responding to and riding out the inevitable uncertainties.

So if you want to go into business, be ready to take on risk and to make it your companion. Learn from it. Adjust. But most important, *be prepared to take action.*

TYPES OF RISK

In my business, we establish our business goals and then align our actions to those goals. We have some boundaries, and if an opportunity arises, we look at it in terms of whether it's within those guidelines.

For instance, I want my company to have sustainable growth. That means we want projects that we can handle comfortably and that offer repeat opportunities. So we ask ourselves: is this an opportunity for sustainable growth, or is this a quick hit that will require a limited but extraordinary effort?

We recently finished a significant renovation to a local library. Here's the thought process we went through before bidding:

- **What's its proximity to our offices?** Yes, it's near our offices, which makes it convenient. Check.
- **Will the weather be a factor?** No. It's winter, but the work is mostly indoors. Check.
- **Do we know the client?** Yes, we've worked with them before, and we like them. Check.
- **Is it bonded?** Yes. Normally, we're leery of those, because some cities have been known to close on them. But this town doesn't, so our bond is safe. Check.

Almost everything about this project fit into our program—it was the right size and duration, it was not going to consume all our resources and force all of us to work eighty hours a week, and it fit with our business plan. It was a calculated risk.

In contrast, a foolish risk would be a big job with someone we didn't know, who might consume all our resources and stretch our budget too thin. If it's a one-off job that carries high rewards, but extraordinary risk, we'll raise the red flag. We want slow, steady, long-term growth; we're not looking to win the lottery. We don't take foolish risks.

Sometimes, even companies that are not standing pat will pass on opportunities. It took me a long time to understand that it's okay to let some opportunities go if you're not ready for them. Early on, I'd get this panicky feeling when we skipped an opportunity, but I learned over time that being methodical and realistic means there will always be more opportunities.

PARALYSIS BY ANALYSIS

At the other end of the spectrum are people who over-analyze. They won't take action until the question is elevated to no-brainer status and the answer is obvious. I love no-brainer decisions as much as anyone, but they are rare and you will lose if you take too much time to calculate your risk. Just as you don't want to be making rash decisions, you don't want your choices to get buried under a mountain of inconclusive research.

Warren Buffett has a fantastic method for avoiding that overanalysis trap. At his annual shareholders' meetings, he makes the CEOs of all the companies Berkshire Hathaway owns compile their accomplishments for the year on one page each. Individuals have trouble whittling down their accomplishments to one page, let alone multinational corporations. But that is what Buffett requires, and he uses those single sheets to decide which companies he's going to sell and which ones he'll keep. He doesn't want to see their books, their annual reports, their profit-and-loss statements. He doesn't want to see any of that shit.

He wants to know, in one page, what's going on with a company. He looks at where they started the year and how they finished it. He may have a lot of one-pagers because Berkshire Hathaway Inc. owns dozens of companies from railroads and utilities to newspapers and candy makers, but no one is accusing Warren Buffett of overanalyzing. The process has worked out pretty well for him: Berkshire Hathaway's annual rate of return (19 percent) is more than twice the S&P average over the last fifty years.

A GUT FEELING

The more experience you have making decisions and weathering your missteps, the more valuable your intuition becomes. Some people think of these gut feelings as some kind of message from God, and while I am a spiritual person, I tend to think of gut feelings as a message from your brain. However you look at it, a gut feeling can be a powerful tool.

A gut feeling can be used by procrastinators as a means of talking themselves out of making a decision or pulling the trigger on a new deal. People who use their gut this way need to ignore it. This is merely your ancient brain trying to protect you in the modern world. Humans were designed for self-preservation from inception. That's what kept them alive in the primitive times. You need to learn how to outsmart your own brain.

But those who are past that intractable point can use their gut feeling to make the right move. It's like a cheat sheet. Your gut will weigh all those factors you've put on your list of pros and cons, and help you get to yes or no. *The job (or business) is something I love. I'll learn something new, which will give me valuable experience down the line. The people I'll work with are smart and have an abundance mindset. My gut tells me to go for it.* Your gut can be a decisive factor.

You need to define the level of risk that is acceptable to

you. Adventure-driven risk like playing blackjack at the casino is at one end of the spectrum, and paralysis by analysis is at the other. Aim for something between these two. One look at these lavish casinos tells you that the casino wins most of the time and usually wins big. The only safe bet would be to bet that by the end of the night the casino will be way ahead.

In business, you have to develop some appetite for risk, but you also need some goals and filters that you can strain the opportunities through:

- Does this opportunity fit my interests and skill set?
- Are there benefits beyond profit?
- Is this my best opportunity for success or is there a better one?

WHY PEOPLE DO NOTHING

Even after a decision is made, procrastinators have dozens of reasons for putting off their work on the new task. They're afraid of failing, perhaps, or the challenge is so big they can't figure out where to start. Some people are just so scatterbrained that they can't organize their thoughts and develop a plan of action.

FIXED MINDSET

Some psychologists attribute the problem of inertia to a person's mindset. Some people go through life with what psychologists call a "fixed mindset," which is when you think you have a certain set of skills and you believe you can't develop new ones. How many times have you heard someone say, "I'm not good at math." This mindset closely resembles the scarcity mindset we discussed in the last chapter. In both a fixed and scarcity mindset, people lack the confidence to take risks and reach for something better. This limits their ability to grow or change their life.

GROWTH MINDSET

The opposite of a fixed mindset is a "growth mindset," which is when you believe you're capable of continually learning and developing as a person. This is similar to the abundance mindset we discussed. When you have a growth mindset, anything seems possible—or at least worth trying. People with a growth mindset enjoy learning and solving new problems.

KNOW YOUR "WHY NOT"

Whatever the reason, it helps if you analyze why you have chosen to do nothing. Here are some questions to ask yourself about that:

- **Are you a perfectionist?** If so, you might set unattainable standards for your work and your business, and this discourages you from trying something new.
- **What am I afraid of?** Entrepreneurs might avoid trying a new initiative because they are worried about losing money. So they play it safe. But the missed opportunities to grow and learn could be more damaging than moving forward.
- **Am I mired in "filler/busy" work?** Many of us are content to put off the big challenges until we get all the less-significant work completed. We feel the need to scratch things off our to-do list. Focusing on low-hanging fruit keeps us from tackling the daunting challenges that could deliver big dividends.
- **Can I picture the benefits of taking action?** If you don't see any value in a project, you're naturally less motivated to work on it. But if you can see how your work ties in with your goals and dreams, you can become very motivated.
- **Do I know how to get started?** When in doubt, make a list. Write down all the steps you need to take to accomplish your goal. Decide which ones can be dealt with immediately and then reorganize the rest of the steps in a logical order. Then get to work!

Another factor to consider is the people around you. Do you have partners who fear risk more than you do? Is your family content with the status quo? If you find yourself mired in this kind of quagmire, read on to the next chapter for help on moving ahead when others want to hold you back.

Chapter 4

THE ENABLER'S GUIDE TO FAILURE

When he was eight, my son Michael was already an outstanding baseball player. He was the shortstop on his Little League team, and he also pitched at an advanced level for his age. Between practices, baseball camps, and games, his world revolved around baseball as well as his favorite professional team, the Boston Red Sox. Michael was deeply drawn in by the game.

Then one afternoon Michael threw a baseball and felt his throwing arm snap. He fell to the ground in tremendous pain, holding his right arm.

The doctors in the emergency room said the bone in his arm had shattered. Just like that. No warning, no simple explanation. The X-ray showed a compound fracture and a large hollow area within the bone, but no one could explain what happened. The emergency room doctors would not rule out the possibility that Michael had cancer. They said we needed to see a specialist.

We had to wait two days to see a specialist at the children's hospital. Needless to say, my wife and I were sick with grief during this time. But we never let our anxiety show to Michael. As far as he knew, he just had a broken arm.

The specialist told us the hollow bone in Michael's arm was not cancer but a birth defect. There was nothing the doctors could do to repair it. With time, the bone could heal, the doctor said, but it would always be hollow and would always break easily if Michael used the arm in a strenuous way.

As I sat in the doctor's office sick to my stomach, it became clear to me that Michael's baseball days were over. Why was this happening to him? This kid lived for baseball, but he could never pitch or play the field again because one strong throw could cause his arm to explode. It broke my heart to think of how he'd have to give up baseball forever. How were my wife and I going to explain this to our little boy?

"Tell him he's a lefty," the doctor said.

What?

"We'll just tell him he's a lefty. His left arm doesn't have any problems, so go out and get him a cool left-handed glove and tell him he's a lefty now. This is totally doable. Technically, anyone can do this," the doctor said.

So that's what we did. We never told Michael he could not do something. We just told him he had to make an adjustment. It will be fun to be different, we said.

Fast forward six years and today Michael is one of the best pitchers in eastern Connecticut. He is the number-one pitcher for Team Connecticut Baseball, and he's got great stuff. What's more, he benefitted from becoming left-handed because left-handed pitchers are more sought after than right-handed pitchers. Additionally, he has the benefit of being a switch hitter as he is still right-handed with all other activities.

Michael's success is a great example of what can happen if you don't enable someone who has had a major setback. No one told Michael that he was finished. No one said his broken arm and hollow bone were an excuse to quit. No one reassured him that it wasn't his fault or that no one would think less of him if he quit baseball. We never said that. We just said, "Hey, you're left-handed now. What do you think? Let's do this!"

Some people might hear this story and think it was a miracle. But it's not a miracle. It's just the story of a young person who didn't accept that some dreams are impossible to achieve.

This book is about how to overcome failure and use it to your benefit. But if you fail, and the people around you rush to reassure you that the setback is not your fault, that you will be okay if you quit and go back to something safer, then you have a problem. You are hearing the wrong message. You have enablers in your life—enablers not of success, but of failure.

It's critical that you identify those people and either avoid them, ignore them, or inform them that you won't tolerate that kind of talk. Your setback may have been someone else's fault, but it's still your problem and you must deal with it.

The first step in dealing with your problem is to tell the enablers of failure that you don't want to be coddled, reassured, or advised to play it safe. You tackle problems. You don't run from them.

WHAT'S AN ENABLER?

Most people think of enablers as people who live with alcoholics or drug addicts. In that scenario, enablers love the addict and want to help them get sober. But in trying to help them, enablers make excuses, cover up behavior, and generally forgive the addicts for their destructive behavior. The addicts avoid the repercussions of their actions, and this allows the behavior to continue. The efforts of enablers to help their loved one actually wind up hurting them.

There are also enablers in business. These are people who discourage your efforts to leverage failures and take responsibility for your setbacks. This kind of enabler does as much damage as the enabler who helps an addict.

The first sign that you have an enabler in your life or career is when you discuss a business or life setback with a friend, associate, or significant other, and they say, "Hey, it's not your fault you failed. The timing was bad." Or they say, "You didn't have enough financing," or "You had no resources," or "Someone cheated you." Whatever went wrong, they excuse it as not your fault. They'll tell you that you are perfectly justified if you decide to quit. They come up with a whole menu of excuses for you to choose from.

That's enabling, and it will end you quickly. Enablers try to make you feel better, but they are actually masking the setback and undercutting your efforts to leverage that failure into something of lasting knowledge and value to you. Enablers don't talk about what really went wrong or how you could learn from the setback. They aren't rolling up their sleeves to help you move forward. Instead, they are patting you on the back and guiding you to the couch so you can lie down and do nothing.

Any dream you had of starting a successful business or any worthwhile endeavor ends when you start believing the enablers around you.

What you need are people who challenge you to overcome setbacks. You want people who hold you accountable, help you identify the problem, and work with you on a solution. You need someone who will say, "Hey man, I feel terrible for you. That was a bad setback, and it sucks. But what can we do to turn this ship around? How are we going to do better next time?"

That's not enabling. That's being resourceful and constructive. People don't fail because they lack resources; they fail because they lack resourcefulness. Steve Jobs didn't have a lot of resources when he started Apple in his garage. But he had a lot of resourcefulness, and look how his work paid off. So remember: to succeed, resourcefulness can be much more valuable than resources.

WHY IS ENABLING BAD?

Enablers tend to be people who have had their own set-backs in life. Instead of learning from those mistakes and trying something else, they essentially quit trying altogether. They dodge risk because they are afraid of failing again, and it makes them feel better when others take the same escape route. So they invite others to take the weak way out. Deep down they are ashamed of their own timid nature, and they want others to join them and share the same frame of mind.

Part of the problem is that enablers *enjoy* weaving their way into your life. They'll infiltrate as far as you'll let them. They lack confidence and use their relationship with you to find validation. They relish being the counselor, coach, or confidante, and they try to get you to compromise your own values and fold into their way of doing things. Good relationships are more a partnership than a comingling—they allow a healthy separation between two people. But relationships with enablers are more binding and stifling.

We all know enablers, but many of us also know people who are practical problem solvers. They aren't interested in blaming others for mistakes, but rather in solving problems and moving on. They don't want to hear about how upset you are, or how badly you got screwed; they want to know what you're doing to solve the problem. In that way, they shift the responsibility to you.

Think about the last time you came face to face with a mistake or a thorny problem. Say you bought a used car from a lot and it broke down three days after the warranty expired. You're stuck with a $2,000 repair bill on top of the car payment you have. There's no way around it; that kind of situation sucks and it's got you very worried about your finances.

An enabler will tell you, "It was the car dealer's fault. They probably knew about the defect and sold you the car anyway. Those bastards." This might make you feel better for a little while, but at the end of the day, you still have a car payment and a repair bill.

A resourceful, problem-solving friend will approach the problem dispassionately. They'll ask questions like, "Did you have the car checked out by a mechanic before you bought it? Did you consider buying an extended warranty? Did you call around to find out if the repair can be done somewhere else for less?"

Of course, you can't do anything about the first two questions now, but it shows you how to think things through better the next time you buy a car. For now, though, it might be a good idea to call around and get some estimates. Also, your friend suggests that you call the dealer. See if they'll do the repair for cost. A lot of dealers will do that because they don't want to get a bad reputation.

The problem solver doesn't waste time absolving or assigning blame. Problem-solvers rationally examine the causes and the potential fix. They don't make you feel like shit, but they do hold you accountable and try to help you learn from your setback. They teach you the value of keeping an open mind and not flying off the handle with woe and vows to never take a risk again. Relax. It's just a setback, just another failure on your path to success. You win because you learn and you're better prepared for the next reversal.

ENABLERS' IMPACT ON YOUNG PEOPLE

Young people who receive enabling advice usually end up suffering the worst results. Making excuses or quitting becomes ingrained in their personality and it haunts them for their entire adult lives. Enablers fill their brain with doubts and fears. Often the enabler is doing so out of compassion or the perception of helping. But it's anything but helpful.

The millennial generation, I'm sorry to say, has suffered more than other generations at the hands of enablers. The millennial generation has grown up in a world where problems are never their fault. There are no winners or losers. Everybody gets a trophy, right? You can have anything you want. When you don't get what you want, you can blame others and mask your emptiness with antidepressants, alcohol, or something worse. Many millennials believe they are entitled to wealth and happiness. They have not been raised to see wealth and happiness as a goal they have to work hard to achieve.

There was a story in the newspaper last week about rich people, including some actors and television personalities, who paid a lawyer hundreds of thousands of dollars to bribe university officials to ensure the rich folks' kids were accepted to such prestigious schools as the University of Southern California, Yale, and Stanford. Talk about enabling.

We need to teach our children about sustainable realities. We need to be willing to tell young people, "You came in last place today. You don't need to beat yourself up for that, but you do have to acknowledge it. What are you going to do next time to try and finish in sixth place or even fourth or third place? What do you have to do to win?"

Enablers who want to "solve" your problem for you steal your motivation to take responsibility and find your own solutions. That kind of theft should be a felony. You might have a participation trophy, but does it mean anything to you?

My wife and I never played the "what if" game with our

son. We would never suggest that it was rotten luck that he was born with a birth defect and had to quit pitching. No, we helped him find another way of doing just what he wanted to do: continue pitching, playing baseball, and getting better at it.

The words you speak as a parent or as someone in an advisory position are powerful and long-lasting, and the wrong messages can grow into a permanent handicap. When Michael broke his arm and we learned about his defect, we could have had a good cry and said, "It's not your fault. Your life in baseball—your passion—is over, due to this random fate." Instead, we kept challenging him and showing him how this event has made him stronger. This wasn't a setback. It was a step up. Left-handed pitchers are rare and valuable, and that's the path Michael decided to take with our encouragement. Try to think of it this way: excuses are lies to yourself.

HOW TO OVERCOME ENABLING

As an entrepreneur or a young professional, you cannot tolerate or entertain advice from an enabler. It's nice to have someone, such as your spouse or a close friend, comfort you when you suffer a setback, but you can't afford to wallow in your self-pity.

At this stage in my life, I have zero tolerance for enablers.

If someone says to me, "Oh, it's not your fault, Mat," I immediately ask them to qualify their statement. "Why is this *not* my fault? How is this *not* my responsibility?" Blaming someone else doesn't solve my problem, does it? It's *my* problem. I'm the only one who can solve it. Maybe, I did, in fact, fuck this up.

As you plan out your new business venture or your new career, keep in mind that a solutions-based thinker is the most valuable person you can work with. You don't want a hand-wringing whiner on your team. You want the person who says, "These five things went wrong last week. We need to figure out how to prevent them from happening again. I've got ten potential solutions, and I'm confident one of them is going to work. Let's try this. If it doesn't work, we can try the next option and then the next. So let's get going."

You just went from a failure to a solution.

If you're going into business, you must redefine your support system and surround yourself with positive, creative thinkers. You need rational partners who are going to help you figure out where you went wrong and what you learned from it. You need answers, not excuses. You want the person who isn't fazed by a setback, but instead can acknowledge mistakes and come in the next day with a plan and the enthusiasm to overcome that misstep. You want the people who work harder after a mistake, not the people who resign and get a job at a bodega or something.

In my business and in many, many businesses, solutions-based thinkers are quick and smart and come up with answers and options. When a customer comes to me and says, "Mat, I've got this problem and that problem and this crazy deadline and this potential penalty for being late, and I don't know what to do," I clear a space on my desk and say, "Well, let's dissect this problem and make a plan."

I don't lean back in my chair and shake my head and share war stories about past jobs that tanked because of somebody's crazy timetable. No. That would be the end of my relationship with that customer. Instead, we break the problem down into its parts and start working on a solution. "Can you accept this and negotiate that? Can you get this delivery moved up two days?" At that point, everyone's brain starts working. Those are solutions.

People don't hire us so they can come in and commiserate about the raw deal they got. They don't come in to hear me say, "Well, I guess you're fucked. I guess you'll be filing for bankruptcy soon." They come to us because we have solutions and innovative thinking. In my business, I surround myself with people who bring creativity to problem-solving.

I don't want a single enabler in the building.

WHAT ATTITUDE SHOULD AN ENTREPRENEUR HAVE?

If you're going to start a new business, you want to develop a solutions-based way of thinking.

Your company is born when you see a potential customer who has a problem or a need you believe you know how to fix. You believe that you have the skills, knowledge, and resources to solve that problem, and you are willing to put together a reasonable plan to solve it.

An enabler is going to tell you that you're crazy. It's too risky, they'll say. Or they'll tell you how much money and time you're going to lose. "It's safer if you just go out and get a job," they may tell you.

Instead, if you take your business idea to someone like me, you'll hear something else.

"Great idea," I'll say. And then I'll ask you some questions:

- Who's your perfect customer?
- How many perfect customers are out there?
- Is your solution a major overhaul of the current system or is it a minor adjustment? If it's a major overhaul, are you sure you didn't overlook a simpler solution?

- How are you going to get your solution to your customers?
- How are your customers going to find out about your solution?
- What's your plan for making this all happen?
- What's your plan for after the problem has been solved?
- How are you going to measure success along the way?

That's an entirely different conversation. I'm posing the kind of questions you'll need to consider before you launch anything. I'm not asking you about the past; I'm focused on the present and the future. You might decide there are too many uncertainties and start looking at other ideas, but at least you won't quit. You'll do something. You'll pencil out your options. You'll be learning and taking action, and when you start looking at other ideas, you'll know what kind of questions to ask. Remember, shortcuts never, ever work.

CHOOSE FRIENDS WISELY

Motivational speaker Jim Rohn once said that we are the average of the five people we spend the most time with. And it's true; our relationships have a tremendous impact on how we think, decide, and appraise ourselves. Additionally, I like to tell my sons that if your four closest friends are idiots, you can rest assured eventually you will be number five.

To be the best person you can be, you must carve naysayers and enablers out of your life and surround yourself with people who can help you get better. One study I read said novices just starting out in business crave positive feedback. Experts, on the other hand, want criticism. Experts use negative feedback to improve.

Experts also know the power of teams. Many problems today are so complex that individuals like you and me can't afford to work in a vacuum. We need the diverse ideas and expertise of others, and you need everyone to understand what success looks like, and what their roles in that success will be. Everyone must pull in the same direction. Great problem solvers get along well with a lot of different people and know how to tap the expertise of others.

You also need to challenge yourself. Great problem solvers are methodical and patient. They know some problems result from several issues, and that it may take some time to solve those issues. They also understand that not all problems require a complex solution.

They embrace these three principles:

- When something is working, do more of it.
- If something's not working, try something else.
- Don't fiddle with the stuff that's working.

With that in mind, let's move on and talk about habits, rituals, and goal-setting activities that will give you the skill and courage you need to embrace failure and turn it into a win.

Chapter 5

CHARTING YOUR ROAD MAP TO SUCCESS

When I was a teenager, I was diagnosed with Crohn's disease, a malady of the large intestine that is extremely painful and disabling. Your body is unable to fight the bacteria, and it leaves you weak and wasted. I don't want to go into the details, but rest assured, it is a nasty disease. When I got hit with a flare-up of Crohn's disease, I would sometimes wind up in the hospital with an IV in my arm. There is no cure for Crohn's, and the medicine they give you is almost as bad as the disease itself.

On one occasion, while riding in an ambulance after a particularly bad bout, I decided I could no longer live this way. I was in too much pain. I never knew when the disease would flare up, and this left me tense and dispirited.

The doctors kept throwing drugs at me, and though the medicine would help for a while, the disease would come roaring back. No one had a long-term answer.

I had just graduated from college, and I wasn't a picture of health. I was forty pounds overweight and working seventy or eighty hours a week. My diet was poor, and I wasn't getting enough sleep. Something had to give.

So I read everything I could find about Crohn's disease and started doing some things to help myself. I stopped eating greasy foods and sugar and cut back on alcohol. I began eating mostly vegetables and did everything I could to boost my immune system. I began working out regularly.

Eating right and exercising became my new habits, and over the next few years, the Crohn's disease faded away. My bouts became less frequent and severe. When I'd go in for my annual colonoscopy, the gastroenterologist said the Crohn's was decreasing. He was amazed. Crohn's typically worsens as you age, but my disease was retreating.

This is why I believe so strongly in the power of setting ambitious goals and developing the habits and discipline to achieve them. It took a lot of hard work to change my diet and start exercising every day, but these new habits pushed me toward a large and rewarding objective and became ingrained in me as a result.

This is why I tell young people entering business to write down their goals and track their progress toward meeting them. It's not enough to just jot something down on a Post-It note and stick it on the refrigerator, although that's better than nothing. You should describe your goals in detail, with pictures, drawings, and diagrams if need be, and the description has to be detailed enough that someone you don't know could look at it and know what you're aiming for.

We talked in chapter two about how written goals can help people change their mindset from scarcity to abundance. We also described how the most effective goals are SMART—Specific, Measurable, Attainable, Relevant, and Timely.

Having vivid goals, however, is only half the battle. If you want to make progress toward reaching those goals, you have to record your efforts and successes, and you have to develop the habits you need to stay on track. These habits must become a permanent part of your life.

THE IMPORTANCE OF GOALS

Stephen Covey, in his book *7 Habits of Highly Effective People*, advocates that people should always "begin with the end in mind." Covey wants you to start every day, every task, or every project with a clear vision of your destination and then to "continue by flexing your proactive muscles to make things happen."

This is a two-step process that involves imagination. First, you must picture where you want to be, and then you have to work to reach that destination. It's the same way a construction project starts. A computerized CAD drawing is created and then emerges from the bare ground with a solid foundation and a framework of girders and so on. We know exactly what that building is going to look like long before we lay the first brick.

It's also essential to have both far-reaching goals (sometimes called Big Hairy Audacious Goals, or BHAGs) and short-term goals. Both sets of goals have to be meaningful and measurable. Your goals can't be "pie in the sky" stuff like, "Make a billion dollars and retire to Barcelona." That's not specific or strategic.

A BHAG, a term coined in the book *Built to Last: Successful Habits of Visionary Companies* by Jim Collins and Jerry Porras, is a goal that seems nearly impossible to achieve but is attainable with extraordinary effort, discipline, confidence, and imagination. A BHAG is, by design, a stretch. For entrepreneurs, a good BHAG will require that you change your work habits, learn new skills, and face some risky challenges.

Deciding on the right BHAG can take some time—weeks, sometimes, and often years—because you must conceptualize a goal that has great meaning to you. The goal has to excite and motivate you, and it has to be big enough to require at least ten years of commitment. It has to be a goal that you can explain simply to others, although you shouldn't expect everyone to share your enthusiasm for the idea. A good BHAG has to feel nearly impossible to achieve.

Once you've settled on your long-term goal, you can start breaking it down into smaller pieces. Remember, you can only eat an elephant one bite at a time, but you have to start slicing off sections and making progress right away. You also must measure your progress by revisiting your goals and sub-goals regularly—either once a week or once a month, depending on how much time you have to work on your BHAG.

Some good examples of BHAGS include the time President John F. Kennedy challenged the nation to put a person on the moon and bring them safely home. Microsoft's BHAG was to put a computer on every desk in every home. Volvo's goal is to ensure that by 2020 no one is killed or seriously injured in one of their cars.

You can see from these examples that BHAGs are a challenge. Success is no way assured, but the goal is so enticing and ambitious that, if you need to, you can quickly get others to share your dream and work with you to achieve it. If you or anyone you work with is unclear about what to do, they can ask themselves, "Does this action move us closer to achieving our overarching goal?" Another advantage of having a compelling BHAG is that it attracts the kind of people who want to reach the same goal as you. Once again, the law of attraction is at work. There are many great books on this principle and it's as real as the ocean.

In my office, I have a nine-by-five-foot whiteboard where we list our big goals and intermediate goals and the progress we're making on them. They are up there where everyone can see them, and everyone is free to add their two cents. One column lists the projects we want to get involved in, and the other column lists the actions we need to take. Finally, we list the results that we achieved. At a glance, someone can see what we are aiming for, how we expect to get there, and the progress we've made toward reaching those goals.

MAKING PROGRESS

Merely having goals is not enough. You must develop the habits required to achieve those goals. Good habits build discipline and give you the mental clarity and physical endurance to focus on your work.

Most successful people and entrepreneurs have healthy habits—they exercise, eat well, get sufficient rest, avoid smoking and drinking, and meditate or pray. These practices work together to refine your attitude, mental fortitude, and physical confidence.

For instance, consider a major league baseball player who practices his swing over and over again so that it is perfect. His body memorizes a pattern of actions that contribute to an ideal rhythm. What's more, he takes care of his vision, builds the correct muscles, and studies pitchers so that he senses when the next pitch will be a fastball or a curveball. He doesn't use a different swing for every pitch. Muscle memory soon takes over and the brain can relax. This is what I think of when Covey talks about "flexing your proactive muscles to make things happen." If you want to be prepared to respond to opportunities or failures, you need that muscle memory. You need that perfect swing and to learn to make adjustments.

BUILDING YOUR MENTAL STRENGTH

As I've mentioned, another essential habit is meditation or prayer. Many are skeptical of meditation, but researchers say meditation brings physical changes to the hippocampus, amygdala, and prefrontal cortex of your brain, improving your long-term memory, courage, and decision-making.

People like Marc Benioff, the co-founder and CEO of Salesforce, and Ray Dalio, the founder of Bridgewater Associates, swear by the practice. Venture capitalist Fred Wilson said meditating fifteen minutes a day for just two months improved his focus. He compares meditation to "the repetitive exercise of the focus muscle in the brain."

A variation of meditation is prayer. I don't want to foist religion on anyone, but I am a spiritual person, and I've found that praying to God brings the same benefits as meditation. Praying slows down and controls your breathing, and this gives you increased focus and perspective. It can help you change your mindset, reduce your stress, and clarify your thinking.

SHOWING GRATITUDE

Meditation and prayer also develop your sense of gratitude. Jeff Weiner, the CEO of LinkedIn, says meditation not only improves his productivity but makes him better at showing empathy and compassion.

Showing gratitude may not sound important to busy business people or budding entrepreneurs, but it's a valuable habit. When you feel grateful, you also feel happier. You don't take things for granted as much, and many psychologists believe focusing on the things you're grateful for can keep you from becoming greedy or feeling entitled.

Showing appreciation and helping others is not only good for you as a human, it's good for your business.

If you are in the habit of showing sincere gratitude, then you are also in the habitat of appreciating your relationships and what others contribute to your life. This wonderful practice enhances your well-being and reinforces your abundance mindset, which we've already shown is essential when starting a business or taking your business to the next level.

Thanking someone, whether it's an employee of yours or a waiter who gave you excellent service, inspires that person to continue that kind of behavior. You are encouraging them to do even more for you. This may sound like a small thing, but it's a game changer. Instead of focusing on what they did wrong—negative feedback carries much more weight than praise—you focus on what they did right.

The number-one reason people quit their jobs is that they don't feel their employer is grateful for their work. You'd think the number-one reason is money, but it isn't. Employees leave because they want to work where their efforts and talents are appreciated and recognized.

You don't need to drop everything and rush out to thank everyone you work with. People can tell if you're insincere.

But if you are humble and genuine about your gratitude, those people are going to feel gratitude toward you. This builds a circle of appreciation that leads to better work and a better work environment. You create an atmosphere where people genuinely want to help each other. It's the opposite of a toxic environment where people put down others to get ahead.

Scientists who have studied the benefits say gratitude strengthens your immune system, improves sleep, and heightens optimism. Your blood pressure might even go down.

If you need to improve in this area, here are a few tips:

- **Each day, jot down a short list of things for which you're grateful.** This practice trains your mind to be on the lookout for praiseworthy things. It also gives you a checklist for the thanks you'll hand out that day.
- **Praise the right way.** Some people like to receive thanks in a private, one-on-one conversation, while others like to hear it in a group setting.
- **Be genuine.** Heartfelt thanks trigger in the recipient feelings of optimism and eagerness. They start looking for more opportunities to help out.

Remember, it's vital to *feel* grateful, but you increase that value by *expressing* your gratitude.

DRAWING YOUR ROAD MAP

Your road map to success takes shape as you meld your goals, habits, and emotional practices into a regular routine. All that you do contributes to your overall success and happiness. Here are some tips for staying on your path:

- **Big goals, little victories.** Develop your ten-year plan (BHAG) but use twenty-minute plans (see chapter one) to reach them. Break that BHAG down into smaller challenges and measure your progress in achieving those milestones. You can start a vision board like I have, or you can get yourself a cool little leather notebook like the poets use to scratch down their thoughts. Writing down your goals and measuring progress is crucial.

- **Stay flexible.** While it's smart to have rituals and muscle memory, don't be too rigid or become a slave to them. Make your habits and attitudes so ingrained that you look forward to them and feel empty when they are missing, but don't lock yourself into an inflexible routine.

- **Eat well.** Eat your vegetables, control your fat intake, and don't consume more calories than you burn in a day. Quit smoking. If your body is strong and healthy, your mind will follow. You'll need both to reach your BHAG.

- **Look inward.** Meditation and prayer are powerful

tools. Try it and keep at it. Get a book on meditation, or read spiritual or religious writings. Give thanks every day—either to your God or to some other higher power—because this prepares you to express your gratitude to those around you. Sometimes giving thanks means writing a check, and that investment will come back to you ten times over.

- **Go all in.** If you are having second thoughts about your undertaking, refine your goal or try something else. You must be wholly committed to the goal or you won't succeed.

- **Control your phone.** I don't want to sound like some-body's grandfather here, but to succeed in business and life, you must restrict your devotion to social media. The world of business is not built on instant gratification. You are not going to find success merely by swiping right. Your interactions with individuals have to be focused and earnest; you can't be thinking about the phone buzzing in your pocket when you're talking to a potential customer. Distractions will kill your efforts.

I think of my own road map as my "too stupid to quit" approach to life. My habits and mindset are so deeply ingrained that I do them almost without thinking. The result is that adversity and fear do not resonate strongly with me. I encounter them and notice them, but I fall back on my road map and keep plowing ahead. As long as I'm on my road map, anxiety is irrelevant; the outcome is the same regardless of whether I worry, and I'll reach my goals faster if I don't waste time worrying. Trial and error is a great teacher.

Anxiety can be powerful, especially for people with actual mental disabilities. But most anxiety is self-inflicted and a lot of people subscribe to that form. Do you know anyone who takes Xanax? I bet you do. Think of anxiety as just a rehearsal to be fearful of a future failure. Why would anyone rehearse to be afraid of something?

Don't worry! You have a plan!

Let's move on now and tackle the topic that gives most young entrepreneurs and rising stars fits: finances. I'll give you the real truth so you can stop worrying and take action instead.

Chapter 6

FINANCES: PERSONAL, BUSINESS, AND THE REAL TRUTH

When my generation entered the workforce, we took jobs at the bottom of the totem pole. We were inexperienced, so we did the scut work because those were the only jobs available to us. I got my first real job washing dishes in a restaurant. I was grateful for the job, but it wasn't exactly high-paying or glamorous.

Today, it's different. When I take my sons around to look at colleges, there are recruiters from all the major companies—Microsoft, Nike, Intel, Apple—right on campus. These companies are conducting interviews and lining up college students for high-paying jobs when they graduate. These companies realize they need to continually bring in a new crop of young people to keep their business growing.

The world has changed dramatically since I was a kid thirty years ago. Today, young people don't merely have a seat on the bus; they are in the driver's seat. I'm not sure they know that, but if you're reading this book and following some of the ideas I've presented here, you should realize that young people control more of the economy and its future than any generation that's come before.

Our economy, with its reliance on technology, communications, and the Internet, is a rich environment for young people. Entrepreneurship is about solving problems, and who better to understand the challenges of an interconnected, technology-driven economy than the young people who grew up with social media, smartphones, and web-based commerce?

Before you can succeed in business, however, you must succeed in your own personal finances. Developing the right habits early on and getting your personal finances in order paves the way for success in business and life. Good personal financial practices reduce your stress about money, build your confidence, and strengthen your resilience for the challenges that come from being an entrepreneur. With a sound personal financial footing, you're more willing to take risks and more likely to make well-reasoned decisions. It's difficult to think clearly about business and your future when you are living paycheck to paycheck and worrying about making your car payment.

GETTING YOUR FINANCIAL HOUSE IN ORDER

Despite their powerful influence on the economy, young people must adopt the right attitude toward managing money—particularly when it comes to saving.

I've talked in earlier chapters about how the Great Depression gave many people a scarcity mindset that encouraged them to protect their possessions and avoid risk. Did the Great Recession of 2008 have the same effect on today's younger generation?

A 2017 Gallup poll showed that before the recession, about half of the people who were under financial stress— living paycheck to paycheck, carrying too much debt, and missing the occasional payment—still enjoyed spending over saving. About 46 percent preferred to save. However, after the 2008 recession, the percentage of those experiencing financial stress who preferred to save jumped to 63 percent, while those who preferred to spend dropped to 35 percent.

Does this mean today's young entrepreneurs have a scarcity mindset? No. Just because you save money doesn't mean you are circling the financial wagons. A scarcity mindset, which we discussed in chapter two, makes you fearful of taking calculated risks and leaves you prone to making damaging, overly conservative decisions. But saving and investing wisely at a young age is never damaging. Instead of fostering a sense of scarcity, saving wisely gives you a firm foundation from which to let your abundance mindset flourish.

There might be other advantages in developing patience and foresight when it comes to saving and personal wealth. For instance, back in the late 1960s, some researchers at Stanford did a study with a group of children from three to six years old. The children were each given one marshmallow and told that if they could wait just fifteen minutes without eating their marshmallow, they would get a second one.

You can imagine what the next fifteen minutes were like. Some kids popped their marshmallow in their mouths immediately. Some fought the temptation as long as they could before caving in. But some waited and were rewarded when the adults came back in the room.

The researchers continued to study this group of children for several years, and found that the children who earned a second marshmallow succeeded in life in many significant ways. They got higher SAT scores than the other kids in the group, were less likely to abuse substances or become obese as an adult, and responded better to stress. Some researchers later challenged the simple results, saying, for instance, that a child's upbringing has more to do with his or her desire for instant gratification than this study would show. That may be true, but the study nevertheless spotlights why self-control, discipline, and patience are valuable skills in life.

The point is that while a scarcity mindset may forestall business success, discipline with your personal finances will help you succeed—now and when you retire. This book is about embracing failure, but when it comes to saving and investing for your future, I wholeheart-edly recommend being intelligent and using the best practices to secure your future. Here are some tips for doing that.

LIVE BELOW YOUR MEANS

This should be your number-one priority. Spending more than you make is a recipe for disaster; it means you never save, you never have a cushion for emergencies, and you live in constant fear that you'll run out of money to live on before your next paycheck. Not having sufficient income to cover your needs also puts tremendous pressure on your relationship with your spouse or partner.

If there is one thing you take away from this chapter, let it be this: *Live below your means and invest the balance.*

START SAVING FOR RETIREMENT IMMEDIATELY

Make it a habit to set aside at least a little bit each month. Put it into a safe, low-cost index fund that tracks the major indices of the stock market. Starting early and saving steadily produce big rewards for your retirement because you can take advantage of a very powerful tool—compounding interest.

TRUST YOUR NEST EGG

Your retirement fund is your safety net. A stable and growing retirement account gives you confidence and a sense of security. Even if your business isn't growing the way you hoped or your career is not as lucrative as you expected, you can feel reassured because you are saving and your money is growing. Think of saving as your side business. This practice also builds discipline, which will be required in all other arenas of your life.

TAKE RESPONSIBILITY

Most young people starting a business or entering the workforce will not have the same retirement pensions our parents and grandparents enjoyed. Most pension plans became history when the federal government created 401(k) accounts in 1978. Now you are responsible for your own retirement savings and managing your own investments. You can't wait until your fifties to worry about this! Start saving now and keep saving.

Don't go into your professional life thinking the government or the Social Security Administration is going to take care of you when you retire. Social Security was never meant to be a person's entire retirement income, and even if you have some healthy Social Security payments coming your way when you retire at sixty-two, sixty-seven, or seventy years old, you are probably going to need additional income to meet your needs.

TAKE YOUR TIME

Everyone wants to be a millionaire before they are thirty. That's a terrific goal and you should work toward it. Make sure you are honest with yourself and make it clear why this is the direction. Most people who are tremendously financially successful become this way as a result of their passion for their work. Financial success is a byproduct of the passion they feel in their career choice, not the purpose.

Think about the long haul. You can become a millionaire by investing a small amount each week into an index fund and letting it grow through the miracle of compound interest. It's not a sexy approach. It's not going to get you on the cover of *Fast Company* magazine. But it is nevertheless a significant accomplishment that provides peace of mind and a sense of achievement. Think of this as another income stream.

AVOID BIG RISKS

Don't chase after the next hot stock or make risky investments that you hope will pay off quickly. Do not obsessively buy and sell assets in an effort to "beat the market" and earn returns higher than the market's overall growth. That's a fool's errand.

Each year a market research firm in Boston does a study of how well investors do compared to the overall stock market. Independent investors always come in below the market average. In 2016, for example, the stock market made close to 12 percent for the year while the average equity investor earned only 7 percent. Why? Because individuals like you and me make emotional decisions. If you just invest conservatively in an index fund tracking the overall market, you do much better in the long run.

EXPLOIT YOUR CONFIDENCE

Smart investing and living below your means gives you

the confidence to take risks elsewhere—namely your business.

If you are always buried in debt, living check to check and not knowing where your next meal is coming from, you will make poor decisions. You won't have the courage (or the credit score) you need to succeed in business. But if you can eliminate the financial fear, you have a confident, abundance mindset that emboldens you to succeed in business. Some people can work effectively under extreme pressure. With their back against the wall. But for most, pressure has a negative effect on the outcome, and if you can plan around it you should do so.

REMAIN HUMBLE

Having a humble attitude helps you succeed in business, and it's equally important as you build your personal finances. You might be able to afford a new Land Rover, but is that really your best investment? Did you factor in the depreciation, insurance, maintenance, and repair costs for that vehicle? Spending too much on a car doesn't reflect an abundance mindset, and driving a used Toyota doesn't reflect a scarcity mindset. Warren Buffett drives a twelve-year-old Cadillac. Do you think he has a scarcity mindset? No. Buffett can drive any car he wants but chooses an old Cadillac because he's humble, unpretentious, and learned long ago to live below his means.

COMMUNICATE WITH YOUR SPOUSE

One of the top ten reasons for divorce is finances, but it's not always a *lack* of money that causes couples to split. More often, couples split because they can't agree on how to *handle* money. One person lives for the day and spends, while the other focuses on the future and saves.

You could write an entire book on how to resolve that basic conflict. In fact, many people have because it's such a prevalent problem. Their advice typically boils down to a few strategies: be honest and open about money, respect your spouse's inclinations about money, establish a budget, set saving goals and spending restrictions, and be patient. That last one is key. If you're the saver and your spouse is a spender, it may take some time for the wisdom of your financial discipline to seep into your spender's consciousness.

In addition, some couples don't share the same overarching goals when it comes to business and careers. For instance, you may want to start a business while your spouse is content to stay in a career with a modest income. That's okay. You can still build a successful business or career if your spouse has more modest aspirations. It's important, however, to understand and respect your spouse's or partner's intentions, whatever they may be.

THE BASEBALL METAPHOR

Confidence is often what separates the good from the great, and a great example of that is found within professional baseball.

If you can make a professional baseball team—I don't care if it's single A, triple A, or the major leagues—you are among the best of the best. All players at those levels are hardworking, disciplined, and skilled players. However, those who make the major leagues are often those who practice more and have more hunger.

These "best of the best" players practice so much that they are profoundly confident they can handle any situation they face. They don't think about failing. They think about the best way to succeed. They don't think about striking out. They think about where to drive the ball when they make contact. They rely on their training.

That's how I look at personal finance. If you establish some rock-hard, consistent habits about saving and living below your means, you develop the confidence to picture success. You don't worry about striking out, because you know how to hit.

In business, you won't get a hit every time. You will fail from time to time. But your personal financial habits give you a backstop. You may swing and miss, but the ball won't get away from you. You know that even if you have failures in business, you'll still have your savings and investments working for you.

With that backstop, you're free to play the game.

SHOWING SOME RESTRAINT

Just as building your savings increases your confidence, decreasing that account can make you feel more vulnerable. That's why it's important not to tap into those funds when emergency expenses arise.

Instead, create an emergency fund for those unexpected expenses. Most financial advisors recommend an emergency fund equal to three to six months of your personal monthly expenses, including your rent or house payment, all your debt payments, your groceries and utilities, and everything else you regularly spend money on.

These funds should be readily available to you, and for that reason, I don't recommend investing your emergency fund in the stock market. You might have bought shares for $150 per share when you invested the emergency money, but the price might be $120 when you need to tap into it. To avoid a big loss like that, keep that cash away from the fluctuations of the market.

You should also have an emergency fund for your business, if you're starting one. It's difficult to operate a business on a shoestring because there are too many unforeseen expenses. Many young entrepreneurs don't realize how much their expenses can fluctuate, so building a cushion is critical.

In business, as well as personal finance, there are two ways you can go. You can live above your means, max out your credit cards, borrow lots of money, and get into a race to the bottom. That's a race you do not want to win. It's a one-way route, and there is no way back.

The other option is to live below your means, invest what's left over in index funds, build your backstop, and work on your business. Now you're on the fast track to success. It's not necessarily a sexy route, and it's not always fun. But it is the path to success, and it's a route that reduces stress in your life, gives you a better quality of life, and puts you in a position to show gratitude, demonstrate humility, and help others.

AVOIDING DEBT

For young people, debt is often a necessary evil. You borrow money for a car. You borrow money for a house to live in. Carefully consider whether you want to take on debts like these. Mortgages make sense for some people who want to build a stake in an appreciating asset—your house—and write off the interest and taxes on their income taxes (though, with the new tax laws, renting is starting to make more and more sense.) Car loans, on the other hand, don't make a lot of financial sense because you are paying interest to purchase something that is plummeting in value. Cars in general are a shitty investment, so try to save up and pay cash for one rather than taking on a six-year loan that locks you into a big monthly payment.

Student loans are probably the biggest ticking time bomb of our time. The price of higher education has sky-rocketed. I personally do not believe it is worthwhile to leverage your future by burying yourself in debt. Think long and hard if this investment is worthwhile for your future. I think you will find it is not. If you put the total cost of your student debt into an index fund and then ran it through any compounding calculator online, you would see an amazing fortune growing instead of the debt you carry. Remember, student debt is the only loan that cannot be forgiven through bankruptcy in the US.

As you can tell, I've never had an appetite for debt. My business has gone through many ups and downs, and at times the only thing that has saved us has been our lack of debt service. I try to pay off debt before I pay myself. Debt is a ticking time bomb.

But sometimes debt is necessary. You might need a small business loan, for instance, and some people take on debt to scale up their business. However, if you have a good business idea, you can scale it without assuming a crippling debt. Too much debt puts you in danger of losing everything if one little thing goes wrong. If you have debt, your highest priority should be to get rid of it.

WHERE ARE YOU HEADED?

At no time in economic history has there been more entrepreneurial opportunities for young people. Microsoft, Apple, Google, and Facebook were all launched by people between the ages of twenty and twenty-six. Businesses need young people like you to guide them through this new economy and to identify the problems that only entrepreneurs of tomorrow can solve. And since you're reading this book, I wouldn't bet a dime against your success in that arena.

As a young, motivated person reading this book, you should understand that there is not as much holding you back as there was for earlier generations. You may not need to wash dishes and do the dirty work like some of us. You are needed and valued, and if you are indeed a problem solver, you are not easily replaced.

However, to fully exploit this opportunity, you must get

your personal financial house in order. Regardless of what you're doing today—whether it's washing dishes in a restaurant or working at a major corporation—start saving. Start living below your means. Pay off your debts. Put yourself in a confident, abundance mindset and then put your energy into exploring your options. Does that future include a lucrative new business? Chances are good that it will, so read on and find out what the next step will be to get you there.

Chapter 7

ENTREPRENEURSHIP 101

When I was in my mid-teens, people often mistook me for someone much older. I was tall, had some scruffy facial hair, and could pass for college age.

One day on my way to work at the restaurant where I washed dishes, I stopped at a convenience store to get some gum. As I came out, two kids asked if I'd buy them some beer. I looked at them like they were crazy and pointed at my homemade bike.

"Look," I said. "That's my vehicle. I ride a bike to work. I'm nowhere close to being twenty-one. Why would you think I would buy you alcohol?"

"Well, you look twenty-one," one of them said. This was a different age, the rules were more relaxed, and this type of thing was commonplace, unfortunately.

I went to work but continued to think about those kids. Then one of my underage coworkers said *he* wished someone would buy *him* some beer. Hmmm. Now I saw a pattern. I saw a need and I saw an opportunity. So I got together with a friend who had a car, cleaned myself up a little bit, and the next day I went into the store and bought a case of beer for fifteen bucks. Then I sold it to my coworker for thirty bucks.

Amazing! I made a 100 percent profit in less than five minutes of work.

So my friend and I started a regular business. I dug out the only suit I owned in the world, bought a pair of sunglasses, and my partner and I started driving around to different liquor stores to buy alcohol. We'd go in at five, about the time the adults were getting off work, and we'd buy booze and then resell it out of the trunk of my friend's car at a 100 percent mark-up. We'd be working at the restaurant and selling beers out of the trunk, making a fortune.

Then one day, a sales clerk at one of the liquor stores asked for my ID and started giving me a hard time. I left, and my friend and I drove away.

When I got home, police officers were at my father's house, sitting around the kitchen table. Did I, they asked, know someone who wore a suit and a tie and bought a lot of beer at local liquor stores?

"Why, no, officers, I don't know anyone like that. Do you have any surveillance video?"

"No. But we have your friend's license plate."

Needless to say, that was the end of our lucrative side business. The suit was retired, and I went back to washing dishes.

This story illustrates the wrong type of business to start. Although we were entrepreneurial—we saw a need and filled it at a profit—this was not our finest hour. We were young, stupid, and desperate, that's all. This is still not an excuse and I certainly do not condone this type of business. To succeed with any start-up, you must be genuine and transparent. Customers prefer to do business with trustworthy people, not phonies wearing cheap suits and sunglasses.

The best businesses are not quick-hit, one-time wonders, but companies that are sustainable and remain profitable when the economy shifts or your customers' interests or needs change. It has to be a business that you believe in. You have to love the work, and you have to be skilled at the work involved. You have to maintain an almost insane level of focus on your customers' needs.

DECIDING ON WHICH BUSINESS TO START

Entrepreneurs launch more than 500,000 new businesses every year. This means that the process of starting a business is pretty clear-cut; there are tons of books, articles, podcasts, and other resources that outline the steps for starting a new business. There's no mystery to it.

What *is* somewhat mysterious is where successful entrepreneurial ideas come from. Where do people get the ideas for all of these new businesses?

The first step is to identify a need. As we've mentioned before, entrepreneurs are problem-solvers; they see something that doesn't exist or doesn't work particularly well, and figure out how to do it better. It's not always necessary to come up with something that's never been done before; it's just as effective to find ways of improving goods or services, or in finding a way to serve an underserved market.

If you're contemplating starting a business, here are some questions to ask yourself:

- **What problem am I solving with this business?** The

problem you identify may merely be a personal need, so it's important to observe and listen to others to see if the problem is broad enough to justify the solution you're proposing.

- **Have I done enough research?** Read about the issue and bounce your idea off as many people as you can. You may worry about someone stealing your idea, but it's unlikely anyone will do that. A more significant concern is the enablers: some people will discourage you from pursuing your idea because they resent your ambition. Don't let them stop you.

- **Is this work that I want to do and why do I want to do it?** On the left side of a sheet of paper, jot down the things you like to do. I like to build things, for instance, and I love numbers. Then, on the right side, write down the things you aren't good at or don't like to do. In the middle, jot down any services or products that would make your life better. Look for a pattern to emerge: Would any of those services or products allow you to utilize your strengths while minimizing your weaknesses? Do you have a passion for the work? Is there a greater cause or rallying cry I hold on this subject?

- **Is it something I would be good at?** Do I have the necessary skills, or should I get some additional training or experience first?

- **Is this something I feel strongly about?** You can start a company merely to make money, but the business will be more successful if you're exhilarated by the work. What's more, your success will grow if your product or service has an emotional impact on your customers. People buy things when the salesperson clearly loves the product or service. The customer thinks, *If this person attaches that much emotion to it, it must be good.*

- **Is now the right time to start my business?** Don't agonize over this question. While it's wise to start your business when the economy is humming and people have money to spend, your customers' pains and needs are often heightened during down times, creating new opportunities for you. Down times are also a great time to buy used equipment and for your business to get noticed.

- **Do I need any technical help right away?** Many first-time entrepreneurs, particularly in the tech field, think they can't get started without hiring experienced coders or designers. This is both untrue and unwise. First, narrow down the intent of your product and develop a deep understanding of your customers and their needs. Meet with potential customers, tell them what you're working on, and get their feedback. Hire experts after you've proven your concept.

- **Do I fully understand my customer?** Businesses start with a clear idea of an audience with a problem. It can be a small audience, but you have to thoroughly understand its pain. Once your solution is viable, use your customers' feedback to expand and reach more people.

SWEAT THE SMALL STUFF

Entrepreneurs must be detail oriented. Many business leaders win because they focus on big success without getting bogged down on small details. However, if you're just getting started, you do need to sweat the small stuff. You must pay attention to the details in your work and your relationships with customers and employees. Sweating the details ensures that you keep your company's standards high.

In our business of construction management, overlooking one small detail can have a devastating effect. For example, building a structure can require pouring hundreds of yards of concrete for the foundation. That concrete has to be tested by a third-party lab every day. But what happens if one day the lab technician doesn't show up, no one notices, and the project continues. Several days later, when you're compiling your reports, you notice that the lab tests for one day are missing. Oh shit. Now you've had several days of concrete poured over that one untested batch, and you have to tear out the foundation and start over.

The tiny detail you missed is going to cost you a fortune.

Therefore, you must stay laser-focused on the details so you can spot an oversight and sound the alarm.

That kind of scenario is true for any business. Do you think Apple products would be as insanely popular today if Steve Jobs hadn't been obsessive about design? Why do you think people rave about flying on Virgin Airlines, but are indifferent or disappointed about their experience on Delta or United?

Always provide the best service or product you can, even if it means lower profits. Keep the bar high. Don't merely meet the customers' expectations—exceed them. Sweating the details also tells your employees that you pay attention and expect the best from them.

Establish controls that allow you to spot even small deviations in your business. For example, we divide our large projects into sixteen divisions of work. Construction managers post expenses against each division. We can instantly tell if we are over budget or under budget in a certain area and can make adjustments as needed. These are small details, but they keep a project from falling off the rails.

HONESTY, TRANSPARENCY, AND GRATITUDE

You cannot have a sustainable business without operating

from a high moral platform. You can't develop a long-term customer unless you are honest and transparent in your dealings with them. Some people believe tough negotiators must be cagey or deceptive, but nothing justifies that kind of behavior. You shouldn't be a pushover, but you can't be misleading or untrustworthy either. If you make a mistake, own it.

As we mentioned earlier, the only way to keep quality workers is to value their work. You must pay them well, but acknowledging their hard work and praising them for it is essential to keeping them. Practice this on your own. Next time you make a purchase or a server brings you a meal offer your deep thanks for the time and attention. See what happens.

The same is true with your customers. Let them know you're grateful for their business. Make yourself readily available to them. Give them your cell number and invite them to call anytime. Chances are they won't call you, but they will appreciate that you considered them important enough to share your personal contact information.

Most importantly, your success depends on your perseverance. The whole point of this book is that you must leverage failure into success. As an entrepreneur starting a business, you are going to make mistakes and hear the word "no" a lot. Accept that and keep moving. Acknowledge your failures and, as the Dalai Lama says, "When you lose, don't lose the lesson."

Eight out of ten start-ups fail within the first eighteen months. That's a lot of failures, but those numbers illustrate just how pugnacious an entrepreneur has to be. It's not unusual for entrepreneurs to start several businesses before they find one that soars, and the main reason they finally reach success is because they've learned so much from previous failures. Those failures raised their confidence, determination, and skill. Next time you meet a successful entrepreneur, ask that person how many times they failed before they struck gold. Most will tick off a litany of failures.

Scientists are just starting to develop new ideas about why some children succeed. They used to attribute success to IQ and test scores, but that's changing. Now scientists are saying that personality traits like persistence, inquisitiveness, and optimism play a much bigger role. You don't need a 1600 on your SATs to do well in business and life. You just need a strong character.

MANAGING RISK

Starting a new business is risky, but you can manage that risk by asking questions, doing research, and consulting experts and mentors. Assess the risk by asking:

- **What precisely am I risking?** Assess how much time and effort are needed to pursue your dream and determine if you have the necessary resources. While you're deliberating this question, assess the risk of *not* doing something.
- **What will I lose if things don't work out?** You don't want to risk your home, your family, or your health, but if all you're risking is a job, some time, energy, and some money, isn't following your dream worth those things?
- **Am I dreaming big enough?** We've talked a lot in this chapter about staying focused on your main idea. It's equally important to look beyond your immediate goals to what a prosperous future might hold. Remember to maintain your abundance mindset and don't overanalyze yourself into paralysis.

DEVELOPING GOOD HABITS

Books give me ideas and inspiration. I wish someone had told me when I was starting out how important reading is to business and life success. Hands-on experience is vital to your growth as an entrepreneur, but books can vastly augment that education and improve your chance of success.

If you want to open a restaurant, there are books about that. If you like to code and you want to build an app, there are books to help you. Remember, success leaves clues. If you want to know how to turn failure into success, I'm sure there's a book out there to help you. In fact, you're holding one of the best in your hands right now.

There is more information at your fingertips today than ever before, and successful entrepreneurs understand the value of tapping into that knowledge. I read whatever I can find about business and construction, but I'm also constantly looking for fresh ideas on how to become a better person.

My goal is to bombard my brain with positive information. There is so much negative information in the world today—five minutes into a newscast and you're ready to kill yourself!—so I choose positive, uplifting messages that help me travel through life. Whatever your business or interests, reading about your passion helps you grow.

ASK FOR HELP

It's wise to find a good mentor. Look for someone who is already established in the business world and understands the market you are moving into. That person could bring valuable perspective to your new business. Many successful people are happy to help, and you might be surprised at how many secrets they are willing to share. Most older people with a lot of experience are flattered

RECOMMENDED READING AND LISTENING

I can't list all the books that have influenced me but here are a few of the books, articles, and podcasts that complement some of the themes we explore in this book.

- Tony Robbins (*MONEY Master the Game: 7 Simple Steps to Financial Freedom*): I also like Tony's podcast for the positive message he always offers.

- Tim Ferris (*Tribe of Mentors: Short Life Advice from the Best in the World*): This book is long but easy to read. You can open it on almost any page and find advice you can put to work immediately. I also admire Tim Ferris's podcast. He's always fun, entertaining, and creative.

- Derek Sivers (*Anything You Want: 40 Lessons for a New Kind of Entrepreneur*): A great easy read that any budding entrepreneur would love. Sivers started CD Baby, an online store for CDs, in 1998 and sold the company eight years later for $22 million. I reached out to him when I began the process of writing this book. He graciously responded and offered his support, and we still are in contact.

- Seth Godin (*Lynchpin: Are You Indispensable?*): A must read. This book really identifies the type of person, employee, or businessperson you should aspire to be.

- Simon Sinek (*Start with Why: How Great Leaders Inspire Everyone to Take Action*): A groundbreaking book that comes from a different perspective that *why* you want to be in business is more important than *what* you do. Awesome read.

- Dean Graziosi (*Millionaire Success Habits: The Gateway to Wealth & Prosperity*): Graziosi is from a similar background as me, so it was easy to identify with his easy-to-read stories and path to success. No two paths are the same.

- Jay Abraham (*Getting Everything You Can Out Of All You Got*) This was a real education on getting specific on how to market, advance, and measure your path to success.

when a young person seeks to tap into their knowledge. Find someone you can call with specific questions and meet with periodically for wide-ranging discussions. If you can't find one, email me at mat@pcm-ct.com.

A long time ago, I realized that in sports, coaching is everything. So I enlisted the services of a business coach who comes in once a week for a couple of hours. We review my goals and document my progress toward them. Between meetings, I work on assignments he's given me. All of this has helped me tremendously. My coach holds me accountable and keeps me from straying off the path, so I recommend that any entrepreneur get one.

There are tons of qualified business coaches operating out there, so look for one who has expertise in your field. There are business coaches who specialize in financial planning, product development, even commercial construction. You can set up a structured program with a coach, or you can keep it casual and more loosely formatted. Some specialize in working with executives while others work with teams. Some coaches will shadow you for a time at work so they can provide more personal feedback.

CONCLUSION

YOU CAN DO THIS

A couple of years ago, we banned the word "unbelievable" in my office. No one is allowed to use that word to describe anything that happens.

In our profession, commercial construction management, nothing is unbelievable. And no matter how bizarre or unexpected a dispute or delay or setback might be, if it just happened, then it can't be unbelievable. And if what happened to you today was unbelievable, what word are you going to use tomorrow when something even more unlikely or ridiculous happens?

I banned the word in order to get everyone's mind away from the idea that setbacks are unfair, unexpected, or should never happen. That's an enabler's way of thinking.

I want people in my office to think of mistakes, problems, or misfortunes as opportunities, not as incredible acts of fate.

In business, you must anticipate that things will go wrong. If you think the problem is unfair or unwarranted, you're giving yourself an excuse to be delayed, angry, or otherwise thrown off course. You can't do that and still succeed. You must treat problems and setbacks as part of the regular course. Problems are absolutely going to happen. Nothing is going to be smooth sailing. Nothing is unbelievable.

I wrote this book to reassure people that fear and adversity are not your enemies. I reached this conclusion through hard work and overcoming my own uncertainty. Back when I started on my career path, I wish someone had given me the advice that fear and adversity are necessities in life and in business. I can tell you now that when you are faced with obstacles and self-doubt, you must objectively recognize them for what they are—just more hurdles to clear and something that should be expected.

No one enjoys fear or failure, including me. I also know there is no growth without fear. On the other side of fear are bliss and success. Whatever you're doing—going to school, starting a profession, starting a business—you must go through fear first.

I hope this book gives you the tools and practices you need to succeed. It all starts with imagining your true goal, picturing a path to it, and then staying on that trail—regardless of how many times you get pushed into the weeds. Ignore the naysayers, develop good habits to go with your strong goals, scrutinize every stumble or fall, and decide how to avoid them in the future.

No one skyrockets to wealth and success. There are no shortcuts. Some triumph faster than others, but that doesn't mean those people didn't put their nose to the grindstone or get knocked over a few times. In business, everyone fails at some point. The winners are those who don't let those failures stop them.

I sometimes compare my business to waging war. As a construction manager, you are always grinding, trying to make forward progress. The process of constructing a new building is fascinating to some people, but it is not magical. There isn't anything romantic about it. It's hard work. It's a process of overcoming one small problem after another. It's about change and change management.

But it's a process that I love, and one I've succeeded at because of the attitude I bring to this type of work. I look at setbacks as part of the job, and each one we overcome makes us stronger and more confident that we will master the next one, and the one after that.

It's an attitude that all successful entrepreneurs must have. To succeed, you must be willing to push ahead and work through all the challenges, little and big, standing in your way. In fact, failure is probably the only thing you can be certain you'll face in life. If you're going to get anywhere, you have to embrace failure, overcome it, and learn from it.

This book hasn't been a pep rally. I'm not handing out participation trophies to my readers. I haven't told you that your failures are not your fault. In fact, the only mistake you can make is to do nothing.

If you've dreamed of starting your own business, get started. If you've dreamed of starting a new career, get on with it.

Don't make the mistake of waiting until you're pretty sure you will succeed. There will never be a right time. Regardless of how long you wait, you will face problems and challenges. Be ready to fail, fail, and fail again, because the route to winning is lined with failures that you must overcome and push aside. Identify what you want to do with your life and take steps every day to get closer to that goal.

Most young people I meet today don't face down their fears. Instead, they do a 180 and walk away from them.

Don't join that group. Instead, laugh at your fear. If you're going to start a business or do great things to help the world, then you will face some obstacles. The goal is to succeed—and to enjoy success, you must conquer your fears and setbacks.

My greatest fear is that I will be on my death bed feeling regret that I didn't try my best at everything I attempted. Regret that I did not do everything I could to help someone who desperately needed help. Regret that I did not live up to my potential. I don't want to die feeling disappointed in myself. I don't want to die realizing that I was my greatest obstacle in life.

You will also find in the end that success is more than driving nice cars and having vast financial resources. Success comes from understanding the value of helping others. And therein lies my goal for this book: to build a generation of young people to be selfless, do great things, help other people, and make the world better in the process.

If you have enjoyed this book, pay me the greatest compliment of all and pass it on to someone else who can find inspiration from it.

I love feedback. If you have a comment or question, I can be reached at mat@pcm-ct.com.

ABOUT THE AUTHOR

MAT PELLETIER is a principal at Pelletier Construction Management LLC, a Clinton, Connecticut, firm that specializes in commercial and industrial construction management, sales, and estimating in the Northeast region of the US. He attended Salve Regina University, where he took courses in law and earned a bachelor of arts degree. He has been in the commercial and residential construction business for more than thirty years. He is married and has two sons, fourteen and seventeen.

CPSIA information can be obtained
at www.ICGtesting.com
Printed in the USA
LVHW092136180619
621676LV00011B/232/P